People

v.

Vonda Fitzpeter

1st Edition

by

Christopher W. Behan
Associate Professor of Law
Southern Illinois University School of Law

ISBN 10:0989666727
ISBN 13:978-0-9896667-2-5
Published by Practice Ready Press
May 2014

This is a peer reviewed publication of

Practice Ready Press

Contact Information:
www.practice-ready-press.com
813-924-4717

Practice Ready Press
6261 14th Avenue South
Suite 201
Gulfport, Florida 33707
chrose3@chrpublishing.com

CONTENTS

Acknowledgments

"The author gratefully acknowledges the assistance of the following individuals and organizations, all of whom were instrumental in helping the development of this case file:

John Beard, Southern Illinois University School of Law Class of 2014.

Danielle DeFranco, Southern Illinois University School of Law Class of 2014.

Lauren Ramsey, Southern Illinois University Carbondale Theater Department.

David Taylor, Distinguished Teaching Professor, Professor of Law and Director of Skills Training, Northern Illinois University College of Law.

Suparna Malempati, Associate Professor of Law and Director of Advocacy Programs, Atlanta's John Marshall Law School.

The Honorable Brocton Lockwood (retired), Energy, Illinois

The Honorable John A. Speroni, Illinois First Judicial Circuit Court, Williamson County, Illinois

William R. Schroeder, Professor of Law, Southern Illinois University School of Law

Thomas Leggans, Assistant United States Attorney, Southern District of Illinois and Adjunct Professor of Law, Southern Illinois University School of Law.

David Lawler, Esq., Marion, Illinois.

Charles H. Rose, III, Professor of Excellence in Advocacy, Director of the Center for Excellence in Advocacy, Stetson University College of Law

Hugh Selby, Barrister, Advocacy and Witness Trainer, Canberra, Australia

The evaluators, jurors and competitors in the 2014 Saluki Invitational Mock Trial Competition, who "beta tested" this case file and helped me revise and improve it."

Christopher W. Behan
Spring 2014

Statement of the Case

During the afternoon and evening hours of July 10, YEAR-1, Vonda Fitzpeter became involved in an altercation with her husband, Gary Fitzpeter. According to Vonda, Gary called her names, kicked her, and pulled her hair because he was displeased with the condition of their home and, particularly, their kitchen. After enduring this abuse, she announced that she was taking the children to a friend's home for the evening and then leaving the next morning to live with her parents in Ohio. Both parties had been drinking alcohol.

According to Gary, he could not let her leave the home and drive a vehicle in her intoxicated condition, especially with the children. After she packed a bag and started to leave with the children, he physically blocked her from leaving the house. When he tried to block her, Vonda physically attacked him by punching him and clawing him. It became necessary to physically subdue her in order to keep her from leaving.

Vonda claims that it was necessary for her to leave the scene by vehicle in order to preserve her life. Her six-year-old daughter, Abby, was in the car with her.

Vonda drove away from the Fitzpeter residence and was apprehended about two miles away, in front of the driveway of her friend Tiffany Clarke. She was bleeding from a laceration wound to her forehead. In addition, she had some bruises on her arm and red marks on her neck and ribs.

Following an investigation by the Calamity Police, Vonda was charged with DUI, child endangerment, and domestic battery. Gary was not charged with any offenses and is, in fact, testifying in this case under immunity.

Vonda has raised the defense of necessity under Calamity law.

Notes Regarding this Case File

1. State of Calamity law is modeled on that of the State of Illinois. Illinois DUI law can be quite complex, so this case will present a simplified version of DUI law.

  a. The DUI charges are based on 625 ILCS 5/11-501.

  b. The defense of necessity is based on *People v. Unger*, 362 N.E.2d 319 (Ill. Sup. Ct. 1977) and 720 ILCS 5/7-13.

  c. For purposes of this trial, we will not involve ourselves with any of the administrative and pre-trial DUI procedures that are part of Illinois law. Assume that all administrative and pre-trial DUI law procedures have been fully complied with. No evidence of them will be presented at trial, and no evidence from them (for instance, the transcript of a Statutory Summary Suspension hearing) is available at use for trial for any purpose.

  d. Jury instructions for all offenses and defenses are included in the case file.

2. The judge WILL permit the defense to raise and argue the defense of necessity, as well as any other defenses that might reasonably be available under the facts of this case.

3. The prosecution MUST call the following witnesses, in any order.
   Officer Terry Taylor
   Officer Pat Palfrey
   Gary Fitzpeter (testifying under immunity)

4. The defense MUST call the following two witnesses:
   Tiffany Clarke
   Lee Austera

5. The defense must also call ONE of the following TWO witnesses (and cannot call both of them under any circumstances). After the prosecution has rested, the defense must inform the prosecution which of these two witnesses it will call:
   Vonda Fitzpeter
   Stanley Jones, Jr.

6. All statements were made and signed under oath. For the handwritten statements, the statements were made in the witness's own handwriting. All witnesses are required to acknowledge their oaths, their signatures, their handwriting, and the ENTIRE CONTENT of their statements.

7. Along with the witness statements, each side has a memorandum from its investigator. The investigator is not available to testify, and the memorandum is not admissible in evidence. **However, all witnesses are aware of the facts in the memoranda pertaining to them and must acknowledge those facts if asked on direct or cross examination.**

8. All documents are authentic.

9. The BAC test for Vonda Fitzpeter done by a pocket police Breathalyzer and the blood test at the hospital were accurate. For purposes of this trial, it is stipulated that Vonda's BAC was .17. No expert witnesses are available for either side to contest or support the Breathalyzer or the blood test, and thus no treatises or materials pertaining to the accuracy of these tests may be introduced into evidence or form the basis for cross-examination. Nor will a judge take judicial notice of the accuracy or lack thereof of these tests.

10. We will use the reasonable inference rule for facts. Witnesses may testify to background information and reasonable inferences not contained in the fact pattern to the extent that such testimony provides context. Reasonable inferences cannot be new facts that could influence the outcome of the case, meaning the added facts are such that would NOT be included in a closing argument. Remember, the primary goal of trying this case is to deal with the facts you have, not to invent material facts to make the case better fit a desired theory. Impeachment by omission is an available remedy for material, non-collateral facts that don't appear in the record, and we will have a jury instruction telling the jury that a proper impeachment by omission means the witness made up a material fact. We will all be better off if no one tries to invent facts at trial. It isn't worth it.

11. July 10, YEAR-1, is a Sunday, *no matter what the actual calendar says*. The 11th is a Monday, the 12th a Tuesday, and so forth. *Neither side may contest this or ask questions designed to suggest the days and dates are otherwise than they are in the case file.*

State of Calamity)

County of Calamity) S.S.

IN THE 1ST JUDICIAL CIRCUIT, CALAMITY COUNTY, CALAMITY CITY, STATE OF CALAMITY

People of the State of Calamity	)	
v.	)	No. 123456
Vonda Fitzpeter	)	

INFORMATION

M.J. Javert, State's Attorney for Calamity County, State of Calamity, now appears before the Circuit Court of the First Judicial Circuit, and in the name and by the authority of the People of the State of Calamity, states that:

COUNT 1

On or about the hour of 8:40 P.M., on or about the 10th of July YEAR-1, in said County and State, Vonda Fitzpeter, hereinafter called the defendant, committed the offense of Driving while Under the Influence of Alcohol, in violation of 625 Calamity Compiled Statutes 5/11-501 of said State, in this, to wit: that the said defendant knowingly and understandingly operated a motor vehicle with a BAC greater than 0.08; and

COUNT 2

On or about the hour of 8:40 P.M., on or about the 10th of July YEAR-1, in said County and State, the defendant committed the offense of Domestic Battery, in violation of 720 Calamity Compiled Statutes 5/12-3.2 of said State, in this, to wit: that the defendant caused bodily harm to Gary Fitzpeter by kicking, punching and biting him in the shoulder; and

COUNT 3

On or about the hour of 8:40 P.M., on or about the 10th of July YEAR-1, in said County and State, the defendant committed the offense of Endangering the Life or Health of a Child, in violation of 720 ILCS 5/12C-5 of said State, in this, in this, to wit: that the defendant endangered the life and health of her 6-year-old daughter, Abbey Jones, when she knowingly and understandingly operated a motor vehicle under the influence of alcohol with Abbey inside said vehicle.

M.J. Javert

M.J. Javert

State's Attorney

Case No 11-11-111

Township of

Calamity County

☑ People State ☐ City/Village of
Of Calamity vs. vs.

Name (Last) Fitzpeter (First) Vonda (M.I.)			Sid #		
Address 8119 Calamity Way	Eyes Blu	☑ Female ☐ Male			
City, State, Zip Calamity City, Calamity, 66666	Hair Blond	Height 5'3"		Weight 125	
Dr. Lic. 867-53-09DL	State	☐ CDL	Exp. Date 3-18	D.O.B 3-28-YEAR-33	

The Undersigned states that on 7/10/ YEAR-1 at 8:50 pm, Defendant did unlawfully operate:

Register No.	State	Year	US DOT #
Make	Year	Color	

☐ 0. Pedestrian 1. ☐ Passenger Car 2. ☐ Rec. Veh. or Truck 3. ☐ Bus 4. ☐ Truck Tractor 5. ☐ Trail or Semi trail 6. ☐ Motorcycle or bicycle 7. ☐ Other

Upon a Public Highway, or other location, Specifically 513 Fremont Street

Located in the county and State Aforesaid and Did Then and There Commit the Following Offense

Calamity Criminal Code

☐ 3-707 Operating Uninsured Vehicle
☐ 6-101 No Valid Driver's License
☐ 6-303 (___) Driving While License Suspended/ Revoked
☐ 11-305 Disobeying Traffic Control Device
☐ 11-501(a)(____) Driving Under Influence
☐ 11-502 (___) Illegal Transportation Alcohol
☐ 11-601(a) Failure to Reduce Speed/Accident
☐ 11-601(b) Speeding ___mph in a ____ mph zone
☐ 11-709 (___) Improper Lane Usage
☐ 12-603.1 Failure to Wear Seat Belt (_) D (_) P

☑ CLCS ☐ Local Ordinance Ch. 720 Act 5 /Sec 12-3.2

Nature of Offense: Domestic Battery

Accident Type: ☐ Driver Injury Only ☐ Property Damage ☐ Personal Injury ☐ Fatal Rep No.
Road Conditions: ☐ Wet ☑ Dry ☐ Snow ☐ Ice
Visibility: ☐ Day ☑ Night ☐ Rain ☐ Snow ☐ Fog ☑ Clear
Method: 0. ☐ H.H. Radar 1. ☐ Plain Car 2. ☐ Radar 3. ☐ A.Craft 4. ☑ Marked 5. ☐ Vascar 6. ☐ C. Signed 7. ☐ Assist 8. ☐ Accident 9. ☐ Other
Notations:

BOND INFORMATION ☐ Full Amount
1. ☐ Cash Currency $________ ☐ E-Bond ________ Auth # ________ ☐ 10%
☐ 2. CC Driver's License ☐ 3. Bond Card No. ____________ Issued by: ____________
☐ 4. Bond Posted on Ticket No. __________ ☐ 5. No Bond-Confined at ____________
☑ 6. Notice to Appear ☐ 7. Promise to Comply ☐ 8. Individual Bond (Full) Amount $__________

WITHOUT ADMITTING GUILT, I promise to comply with the terms of this Ticket and Release
Signature Vonda Fitzpeter

Circuit Court Location and Date
Address /
Courthouse Calamity City Courthouse

City Calamity City Zip 66666 On 12-12 At 9:00 am

☑ Court Appearance Required ☐ No Court Appearance Required

Case No 11-11-111

Township of

Calamity County

☑ People State ☐ City/Village of
Of Calamity vs. vs.

Name (Last) Fitzpeter (First) Vonda (M.I.)			Sid #		
Address 8119 Calamity Way	Eyes Blu	☑ Female ☐ Male			
City, State, Zip Calamity City, Calamity, 66666	Hair Blond	Height 5'3"		Weight 135	
Dr. Lic. 867-53-09DL	State	☐ CDL	Exp. Date 3-18	D.O.B 3-28-YEAR-33	

The Undersigned states that on 7/10/ YEAR-1 at 8:50 pm, Defendant did unlawfully operate:

Register No.	State	Year	US DOT #
Make	Year	Color	

☐ 0. Pedestrian 1. ☐ Passenger Car 2. ☐ Rec. Veh. or Truck 3. ☐ Bus 4. ☐ Truck Tractor 5. ☐ Trail or Semi trail 6. ☐ Motorcycle or bicycle 7. ☐ Other

Upon a Public Highway, or other location, Specifically 513 Fremont Street

Located in the county and State Aforesaid and Did Then and There Commit the Following Offense

I.V.C. 625 CCCS 5/ :

☐ 3-707 Operating Uninsured Vehicle
☐ 6-101 No Valid Driver's License
☐ 6-303 (___) Driving While License Suspended/ Revoked
☐ 11-305 Disobeying Traffic Control Device
☐ 11-501(a)(____) Driving Under Influence
☐ 11-502 (___) Illegal Transportation Alcohol
☐ 11-601(a) Failure to Reduce Speed/Accident
☐ 11-601(b) Speeding ___mph in a ____ mph zone
☐ 11-709 (___) Improper Lane Usage
☐ 12-603.1 Failure to Wear Seat Belt (_) D (_) P

☑ ILCS ☐ Local Ordinance Ch. 720 Act 5 /Sec 12C-5

Nature of Offense: Child Endangerment

Accident Type: ☐ Driver Injury Only ☐ Property Damage ☐ Personal Injury ☐ Fatal Rep No.
Road Conditions: ☐ Wet ☑ Dry ☐ Snow ☐ Ice
Visibility: ☐ Day ☑ Night ☐ Rain ☐ Snow ☐ Fog ☐ Clear
Method: 0. ☐ H.H. Radar 1. ☐ Plain Car 2. ☐ Radar 3. ☐ A.Craft 4. ☑ Marked 5. ☐ Vascar 6. ☐ C. Signed 7. ☐ Assist 8. ☐ Accident 9. ☐ Other
Notations:

BOND INFORMATION ☐ Full Amount ☐ 10%
1. ☐ Cash Currency $________ ☐ E-Bond ________ Auth # ________
☐ 2. CC Driver's License ☐ 3. Bond Card No. ____________ Issued by: ____________
☐ 4. Bond Posted on Ticket No. __________ ☐ 5. No Bond-Confined at ____________
☑ 6. Notice to Appear ☐ 7. Promise to Comply ☐ 8. Individual Bond (Full) Amount $__________

WITHOUT ADMITTING GUILT, I promise to comply with the terms of this Ticket and Release
Signature X Vonda Fitzpeter

Circuit Court Location and Date
Address /
Courthouse Calamity City Courthouse

City Calamity City Zip 66666 On 12-12 At 9:00 am

☑ Court Appearance Required ☐ No Court Appearance Required

Case No 11-11-111

Township of

Calamity County

☑ People State ☐ City/Village of
Of Calamity vs. vs.

Name Sid #

(Last) Fitzpeter (First) Vonda (M.I.)

Address	Eyes	☑ Female	
8119 Calamity Way	Blue	☐ Male	
City, State, Zip Calamity City, Calamity, 66666	Hair Blonde	Height 5'3"	Weight 125

Dr. Lic.	State	CDL	Exp. Date	D.O.B
867-53-09DL		☐ CDL	3-18	3-28-YEAR-33

The Undersigned states that on 7/10/ YEAR-1 at 8:50 pm, Defendant did unlawfully operate:

Register No.	State	Year	US DOT #
A25 1758	Calamity		

Make	Year	Color
Chevy	08	Silver

☐ 0. Pedestrian ☐ 1. Passenger Car ☑ 2. Rec. Veh. or Truck ☐ 3. Bus ☐ 4. Truck Tractor ☐ 5. Trail or Semi trail ☐ 6. Motorcycle or bicycle ☐ 7. Other

Upon a Public Highway, or other location, Specifically 513 Fremont Street

Located in the county and State Aforesaid and Did Then and There Commit the Following Offense

C.V.C. 625 CCCS 5/ :

☐ 3-707 Operating Uninsured Vehicle
☐ 6-101 No Valid Driver's License
☐ 6-303 (___) Driving While License Suspended/ Revoked
☐ 11-305 Disobeying Traffic Control Device
☑ 11-501(a)(1) Driving Under Influence
☐ 11-502 (___) Illegal Transportation Alcohol
☐ 11-601(a) Failure to Reduce Speed/Accident
☐ 11-601(b) Speeding ___mph in a ____ mph zone
☐ 11-709 (___) Improper Lane Usage
☐ 12-603.1 Failure to Wear Seat Belt (_) D (_) P

☑ CLCS ☐ Local Ordinance Ch. ___________ Act__________ /Sec

____

Nature of Offense: Preliminary BAC (Pocket Breathalyzer) .17. Operating motor vehicle.

Accident Type: ☐ Driver Injury Only ☐ Property Damage ☐ Personal Injury ☐ Fatal Rep No.
Road Conditions: ☐ Wet ☑ Dry ☐ Snow ☐ Ice
Visibility: ☐ Day ☑ Night ☐ Rain ☐ Snow ☐ Fog ☑ Clear
Method: 0. ☐ H.H. Radar 1. ☐ Plain Car 2. ☐ Radar 3. ☐ A.Craft 4. ☑ Marked 5. ☐ Vascar 6. ☐ C. Signed 7. ☐ Assist 8. ☐ Accident 9. ☐ Other
Notations:

BOND INFORMATION ☐ Full Amount ☐ 10%
1. ☐ Cash Currency $________ ☐ E-Bond ________ Auth # ________
☐ 2. CC Driver's License ☐ 3. Bond Card No. ________________ Issued by: _________________
☐ 4. Bond Posted on Ticket No. ___________ ☑ 5. No Bond-Confined at Calamity City Jail
☑ 6. Notice to Appear ☐ 7. Promise to Comply ☐ 8. Individual Bond (Full) Amount $____________

WITHOUT ADMITTING GUILT, I promise to comply with the terms of this Ticket and Release
Signature X Vonda Fitzpeter

CALAMITY CITY POLICE DEPARTMENT	Case Number: 11-CF-111

Offense (s): Domestic Battery Reporting Date: 7/11/YEAR-1 Time: 2:40 am

ILCS # (s): ______________ Occurred – Date/Time: 7/10/YEAR-1 8:50 pm

Location Occurrence: 8119 Calamity Way

Code: Victim = V Reporting Party = R Discovered Crime = D Witness = W Parent = P

Last Name: Fitzpeter First: Gary MI: T Code: V Juvenile: _____

Race: W Sex: M Age: 34 DOB: 7-22-YEAR-34 Ph. (__) ______ - ______

Address: 8119 Calamity Way Bus. Ph. #: ______

Last Name: Jones First: Abbey MI: E Code: _____ Juvenile: X

Race: W Sex: F Age: 6 DOB: 1-19-YEAR-6 Ph. (__) ______ - ______

Address: ______ Bus. Ph. #: ______

Last Name: Fitzpeter First: Stan MI: F Code: _____ Juvenile: X

Race: W Sex: M Age: 2 DOB: 3-25-YEAR-2 Ph. (__) ______ - ______

Address: ______ Bus. Ph. #: ______

SUSPECT / ARREST INFORMATION

Key: Brown = BRO, Blue = BLU, Black = BLK, Hazel = HZL, Blonde = BLN, Red = RED, Last Name Unknown = LNU, First Name Unknown = FNU, Unknown = UNK, Code: Suspect Only = S, Suspect Arrest = A

Last Name: Fitzpeter First: Vonda MI: A Code: A Juvenile: _____

Race: W Sex: F Age: 33 DOB: 3-28-YEAR-33 Hair: Blond Eyes: Blu Ht. 5'3" Wt. 125

Address: 8119 Calamity Way Relationship: Spouse

Last Name: ______ First: ______ MI: _____ Code: _____ Juvenile: _____

Race: _____	Sex: _____	Age: _____	DOB: _________	Hair: _____	Eyes: _____	Ht. ____	Wt. ____
Address: ______________________________					Relationship: ________________		

SUSPECT VEHICLE INFO:	
Reporting Officer: T. Taylor Date: 7/11/YEAR-1	Supervisor
Distribution: ______________________ Recorded: ____________	
EVENT: Refer to enclosed narrative ________________________________ ________________________________	

11-CF-111 Supplemental
7-10-YEAR-1

On July 10, YEAR-1 at approximately 8:50 pm I, Tracy Taylor, patrolman for the city of Calamity was dispatched to 8119 Calamity Way in reference to a domestic dispute. Dispatch advised the female had left the residence with a small child in a silver Chevy Cobalt. As I proceeded westbound on Oak Street I observed a vehicle matching that description pass by me in the 500 block. I proceeded behind the vehicle. The vehicle turned south onto Main St., then east onto Pine and back south onto Fremont St. The vehicle pulled into the driveway of 513 Fremont Street. As the vehicle came to a stop a female exited. The female was bleeding from the area above her right eye. The female was crying and began to stumble around the driveway of the residence. I asked the adult female to calm down and to explain what happened. The female stated that her and her husband got into a physical altercation and that he threw her on the garage floor. The female advised her name was Vonda Fitzpeter and that her friend Tiffany lived at 513 Fremont Street. I notified Calamity City EMS and asked them to respond to my location. Fitzpeter continued crying and stating that her husband threw her on the garage floor and choked her. Fitzpeter advised that her 6 year old daughter and her 2 year old son were still at the residence. The female appeared to be very intoxicated. As I spoke with Fitzpeter I could smell a very strong odor of alcoholic beverage coming from her breath. I asked Fitzpeter if she had been drinking. She advised she had. I did not think it was necessary to perform field sobriety tests because of Fitzpeter's obviously intoxicated condition, but I did ask her if she would consent to a Breathalyzer test. She did provide verbal consent, and I used a pocket Breathalyzer that had been calibrated at the beginning of my shift. She registered a .17 BAC on the pocket Breathalyzer.

At this time Sgt. Pelfrey arrived on scene and observed Fitzpeter's injuries and intoxicated condition.

A female child exited the rear of the vehicle. The child identified herself as Abbey Jones and advised that she was six years old and that Vonda Fitzpeter was her mother. Fitzpeter said, "I thought Daddy made you stay at home!" To the undersigned, she did not seem to be surprised that the child was in the car. She seemed to be trying to act surprised.

Sgt. Pelfrey then left the scene and attempted to locate Fitzpeter's husband at their residence 8119 Calamity Way. Calamity City EMS arrived on scene and began evaluating Fitzpeter. In addition to the laceration on her face, she had some bruises on her arms and legs and red marks on her neck and ribs. I did not take photographs of her injuries because EMS indicated she would be transported to the hospital for evaluation. In my experience, photographs such as this are taken at the hospital.

I proceeded to look through Fitzpeter's vehicle for identification and emergency contact information. I observed a half emptied bottle of vodka lying in the front passenger's seat. The bottle was very cold and had condensation on the outside. I also observed one unopened bottle of Wild Turkey lying on the front passenger's floorboard. There were several prescription medication bottles in the front passenger's seat. As I looked through the medications I observed a small plastic bag containing what appeared to be mushrooms lying in the front passenger's seat. I also observed a small bag containing a large amount of money. There were also several bills thrown throughout the front seat area of the vehicle. At that time I collected the open alcohol bottles, money, medications and bag of mushrooms and secured them in the front seat of my patrol vehicle.

Calamity City EMS advised they were taking Fitzpeter to the Calamity City ER for further evaluation. Before the EMS vehicle left the scene, Fitzpeter asked me if I could leave Abbey with her friend Tiffany, who resided at 513 Fremont. By this time I had received a radio request from Sgt Pelfrey to take the child into protective custody and transport her to 8119 Calamity Way, so I told Vonda Fitzpeter I could not leave the child. She cursed and said that Gary Fitzpeter was "a bastard" and "asshole" and that he was trying to take her children away from her.

I proceeded to join Sgt. Pelfrey at 8119 Calamity Way. Abbey Jones was in the back of the car. At this time, I did not try to initiate any conversation with the child. Abbey Jones did ask me if her mother would be okay and I advised that she was receiving medical treatment. Abbey Jones then advised that Daddy and Mommy had gotten into a fight. We did not have any further conversation.

Upon arrival at 8119 Calamity Way I released Abbey Jones to Gary Fitzpeter. I collected the victim's information as well as the two juvenile's information. Gary Fitzpeter was given a list of his victim's rights as well as information on how to obtain an order of protection. I obtained a written statement from him at the time.

Tracy Taylor
Badge #9999

Case Number: 11-11-111
Date: July 11, YEAR-1
Offenses: Possession of a Controlled Substance, Domestic Battery, DUI, Illegal Transportation of Alcohol; Child Endangerment
Suspect: Vonda Fitzpeter

On July 10, YEAR-1 at approximately 8:50 pm I was assigned to normal supervisory duties with the Calamity City Police Department when I was informed of a child passenger with an intoxicated driver in a silver Chevy Cobalt leaving 8119 Calamity Way by the Calamity Sheriff's Office Telecommunicator. I immediately proceeded in the general direction given along with Officer Tracy Taylor. After approximately one minute after the initial dispatch, Officer Taylor located a vehicle matching the description given and attempted to initiate a stop in the vicinity of Main and Pine.

The silver Chevy Cobalt continued to a driveway of a residence at 513 Fremont and stopped. As I was approaching the vehicle and Officer Taylor, I observed a white female exit the vehicle and stagger toward Officer Taylor. The white female had a laceration above her eye and had blood on her shirt and face. I overheard the white female state her husband threw her on the floor and struck her repeatedly.

At this time I departed the scene at 513 Fremont Street and proceeded to the residence at 8119 Calamity Way. Just before I left I observed a young female child exit the rear of the silver Chevy Cobalt. The white adult female seemed said, "What are you doing in the car? I thought you were with Daddy?" The adult female was acting surprised, but it did not seem convincing to me.

When I arrived at 8119 Calamity Way, I met with Gary Fitzpeter at this location and observed he had blood on his face and shirt. Gary additionally had visible abrasions on his elbows and foot. I asked Gary to describe what happened. Gary stated he had been arguing with his wife, Vonda Fitzpeter, off and on through the night primarily because of her drinking. At one point Vonda allegedly created a huge mess in the kitchen and took apart the oven.

At approximately 8:40 pm, Vonda allegedly attempted to place their two children in the silver Chevy to leave the residence. Gary stated he intervened and removed the children from the vehicle out of concern of her level of intoxication. At this point, Vonda began to attack Gary from behind striking him several times as he placed the children in the house. Gary stated he attempted to talk to Vonda in the garage at which point she again attacked him and fell to the floor on at least two occasions. Gary stated after Vonda fell the second time he attempted to subdue her in order to calm her down. He did subdue her by holding her down on the ground. After Vonda asked to be let up to get some air and be left alone, Gary stated he allowed her up at which point Vonda got into the car and left the residence. He indicated that he did not find out until after she left that Abbey had gotten into the car.

After receiving Gary's initial verbal statement, I contacted Officer Taylor via cell phone to speak with him regarding Vonda's account. Officer Taylor stated Vonda told him Gary attacked her and threw her to the ground. Officer Taylor advised the Calamity City Fire Department was on scene to transport Vonda from 513 Fremont Street. Officer Taylor additionally stated Vonda was extremely intoxicated and he had observed one bottle of vodka and one bottle of Wild Turkey bourbon on the front passenger floor board of the vehicle and a clear plastic bag sitting on the front passenger seat containing what appeared to be mushrooms. A small bag containing a significant amount of U.S. currency was also present in the vehicle. I instructed Officer Taylor to place Abbey Jones in protective custody and to transport her to the residence at 8119 Calamity Way.

At this time I returned to the scene to take pictures of the scene and Gary. The kitchen was in disarray. The refrigerator was pulled away from the wall and the drawer under the oven was in front of the oven. There were pots and pans all over the kitchen and a couple of piles of dust and debris.

A pool of blood was visible on the garage floor with several points of spatter in the general vicinity. The spatter observed on the floor had no indications of horizontal velocity. Based on the size of the spatter and pattern, it appeared the drops were from a relatively low height consistent with Gary's account of Vonda being prone on the floor for a short duration. Small amounts of spatter were visible on a chest style freezer and at the threshold entering into the living space of the residence.

I took digital photographs of everything with my personal cellular telephone. I did not call in a department photographer, because department policy permits us to use our personal cellphone cameras for these pictures. I also took pictures of Gary Fitzpeter's injuries.

Upon his arrival at 8119 Calamity Way, Officer Taylor turned over the alcohol bottles, cash and mushrooms to me. I placed them in my patrol vehicle. I then spoke with Abbey Jones away from any other involved parties and asked her what happened. Abbey stated "Mommy hit Daddy and then she fell down." I asked Abbey if she observed Gary push Vonda to the ground and she again stated Vonda fell. I asked Abbey if she wanted to go to Ohio or stay at home with Gary and she replied "I want to stay here with Daddy."

After returning Abbey Jones and the bag of cash to Gary, I proceeded to the Calamity City Police Department to collect some documentation and then drove to the Calamity City ER to speak with Vonda. I found Vonda lying in bed speaking to a person she advised was her father on the phone. I observed Vonda to have red watery eyes, slurred speech and a strong odor of alcoholic beverages was present in the room. Vonda had a bandage above her right eye and patches of dried blood on her face. A nurse was attending to her as I entered the room. Once the nurse was done, I informed Vonda I would be conducting a Domestic Battery investigation and would read her the Miranda Warning before asking any questions.

After reading the Miranda Warning, Vonda stated she understood her rights and signed the document stating the same. I asked Vonda to describe what happened. Vonda stated she and Gary had been arguing throughout the evening. Vonda stated during the course of the argument she became concerned for her safety and intended on leaving to her friend's residence at 513 Fremont Street and then departing to Ohio in the morning with the children. Vonda alleged Gary Fitzpeter grabbed her by the throat and threw her to the ground causing the laceration to her head. Vonda then stated she fought her way out of the garage and left the residence in the silver Chevy.

Vonda stated Gary was violent on previous occasions and pointed to several bruises on her legs. The bruises were dark brown in color and were not recent. I asked Vonda to allow me to inspect her neck and throat area. There was no discoloration or any bruising evident on her neck. There was some redness but this was consistent with flushed skin due to intoxication and not, in my opinion, from being choked. I asked Vonda about the open alcohol containers on the floorboard of the vehicle. Vonda denied any knowledge of the alcohol containers and alleged Gary "must have planted them there" without her knowledge. I then asked Vonda about the mushrooms on her passenger seat at which time she stated the mushrooms were for recreational use for her and her husband but she denied placing them in the vehicle.

I asked Vonda if she was under the influence of the mushrooms. Vonda denied using the mushrooms and stated "take my blood and I'll prove it." At this time I issued Vonda the Warning to Motorist and informed her I suspected she had been operating her vehicle under the influence of alcohol. Vonda stated she had been drinking but "not that much" and "I haven't eaten since breakfast so that will make a difference." At this time an Imaging Technician entered the room and stated he required Vonda to take some images of her head and spine. Vonda was taken out of the room for approximately 20 minutes before being returned.

Once Vonda was back in the room, I asked her if she was still consenting to a blood draw. Vonda stated she would to prove she had not consumed any mushrooms. I then requested her attending nurse, a Lee Austera, to draw her blood in my presence as Vonda had consented. Once the blood was drawn, Lee Austera sealed the kit per the instructions. Just prior to the blood draw, the attending physician stated her initial BAC from Officer Taylor's Breathalyzer was .17 when she was admitted to the ER.

Once Vonda was discharged from the ER, I informed her she was under arrest for the violations listed above and transported her to the Calamity City Jail for confinement. Upon arriving in the booking area, I was informed by SGT J.W. Weatherford they would not accept Vonda for confinement due to no documentation specifically releasing her to be incarcerated. Vonda's discharge papers were presented and I was informed they were not sufficient for incarceration due to department policy. At this time I returned to my patrol vehicle and released HF from the restraints and transported her back to 513 Fremont Street.

Vonda was released on a Notice to Appear bond after receiving consent from the residents to stay there. She was informed to not return to the residence at 8119 Calamity Way for 72 hours. Vonda was provided a statement form if she intended on submitting a written statement. After releasing her, I departed and resumed my regular patrol duties.

On July 11, YEAR-1 at approximately 8:45 pm, I returned to the residence at 8119 Calamity Way to speak with G. Fitzpeter and to check on the welfare of the children. Gary gave me a completed statement form but still declined to sign a formal request for prosecution at this time. Gary stated he had an appointment with a lawyer to request additional advice on options for a course of action. No further at this time.

SGT Pat Pelfrey

I responded to a call of *Child Endangerment* at *8119 Calamity Way*

CALAMITY CITY POLICE DEPARTMENT		DOMESTIC VIOLENCE SUPPLEMENTAL
Victim's Name *Gary Fitzpeter*	Date of Birth *7-22-(YEAR-34)*	WCSD Case No.

I found the victim — The victim displayed the following emotional and physical conditions:

VICTIM

- ☐ Angry
- ☐ Apologetic
- ☐ Crying
- ☐ Fearful
- ☐ Hysterical
- ☑ Calm
- ☐ Afraid
- ☐ Irrational
- ☐ Nervous
- ☐ Threatening
- ☐ Other: Explain

- ☐ Comp of Pain
- ☑ Bruise (s)
- ☑ Abrasion (s)
- ☐ Minor Cut (s)
- ☐ Laceration (s)
- ☐ Fracture (s)
- ☐ Concussion (s)
- ☐ Other: Explain

Physical: *Victim had a bite mark on chest, abrasions on elbows and top of foot. A scratch on right cheek.*

Emotional: *Victim was calm but visually shaken from event*

SUSPECT

- ☐ Angry
- ☐ Apologetic
- ☑ Crying
- ☐ Fearful
- ☑ Hysterical
- ☐ Calm
- ☐ Afraid
- ☐ Irrational
- ☐ Nervous
- ☐ Threatening
- ☐ Other: Explain

- ☐ Comp of Pain
- ☐ Bruise (s)
- ☐ Abrasion (s)
- ☐ Minor Cut (s)
- ☑ Laceration (s)
- ☐ Fracture (s)
- ☐ Concussion (s)
- ☐ Other: Explain

Crime Scene: *Pool of blood on garage floor with spatter consistent with low vertical fall, blood smears on doorway with drops through a hallway, victim's shirt had blood on left sleeve toward the rear of the arm, child had small amount of blood on the back of a shirt*

Relationship Between Victim and Suspect

Mark all that apply

- ☑ Spouse
- ☐ Former Spouse
- ☐ Cohabitants
- ☐ Former Cohabitants
- ☐ Dating/Engaged
- ☐ Former Dating
- ☐ Same Sex
- ☐ Emancipated Minor
- ☐ Parent of Child from Relationship

Length of Relationship

4 year(s) *1* month(s)

If Applicable, Date Relationship Ended: ____________

Prior history of domestic violence? ☐ Yes ☐ No

Prior history of violence documented? ☐ Yes ☐ No

Number of Prior Incidents: *Unk.* ☐ Minor ☐ Serious

Case Number(s) *N/A*

Investigating Agency *N/A*

MEDICAL TREATMENT ☐ None ☐ Will seek own doctor ☐ First aid ☐ Paramedics ☐ Hospital ☑ Refused Medical aid	Paramedics at scene: ☑ Yes ☐ No Unit Number: ________________ Name(s) ID #: ______________________________	Hospital: ____________________ Attending Physician(s): ________ ____________________________ ____________________________

EVIDENCE COLLECTED From: ☑ Crime Scene ☑ Hospital ☐ Other: Explain Photos: ☐ Yes ☐ No Number: ____________ Type: ☐ 35mm ☐ Polaroid Taken by: _P Pelfrey, T. Taylor______ Describe all Photographs Photos of victim's injuries: ☑ Yes ☐ No Photos of suspect's injuries: ☐ Yes ☑ No Weapon used during incident: ☐ Yes ☑ No Type of weapon used: _N/A______________ Weapon(s) impounded: ☐ Yes ☑ No Firearm(s) impounded for safety: ☐ Yes ☑ No Property Tag Number: ________________	DESCRIBE ALL EVIDENCE AND DISPOSITION _Digital Photographs – Retained electronically_______________ _1 bottle Stoika Vodka – Destroyed _1 bottle Wild Turkey bourbon – Destroyed_______________ _1 plastic bag containing what appears to be illegal mushrooms- destroyed___________ _1 DUI blood kit – Taken in emergency room by doctor and submitted for analysis_______________

Witnesses Present During Domestic Violence? ☑ Yes ☐ No
Statement(s) taken? ☐ Yes ☑ No

Children Present During Domestic Violence? ☑ Yes ☐ No Number Present? _____ Age(s) _____
All Names of Children: _Abbey Jones, Stan Fitzpeter____________________

Statement(s) Taken? ☐ Yes ☑ No
Witness Info Listed? ☑ Yes ☐ No

Order of Protection ☐ Yes ☑ No ☐ Current ☐ Expired Type: ☐ Emergency ☐ Temporary ☐ Permanent Issuing Court: ____N/A________________ Order or Docket Number: ___N/A__________	Victim Given: ☑ Domestic Violence Information Sheet ☑ Crime Case Number ☑ Domestic Violence Unit Telephone Number

Reporting Officer	ID Number	Div. Watch	Date & Time	Approved by:
P. Pelfrey	# 8888			

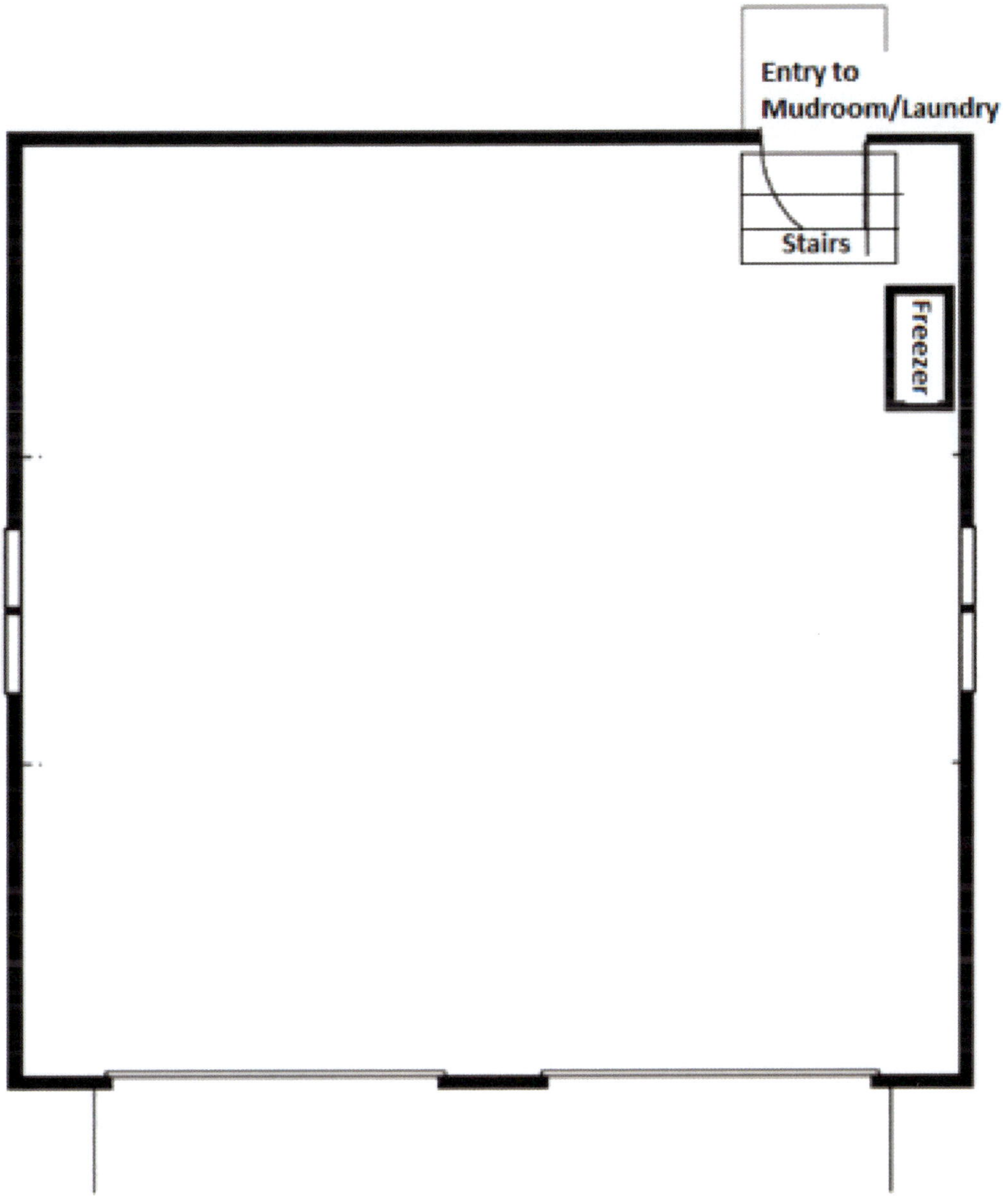
Entry to
Mudroom/Laundry
Stairs
Freezer

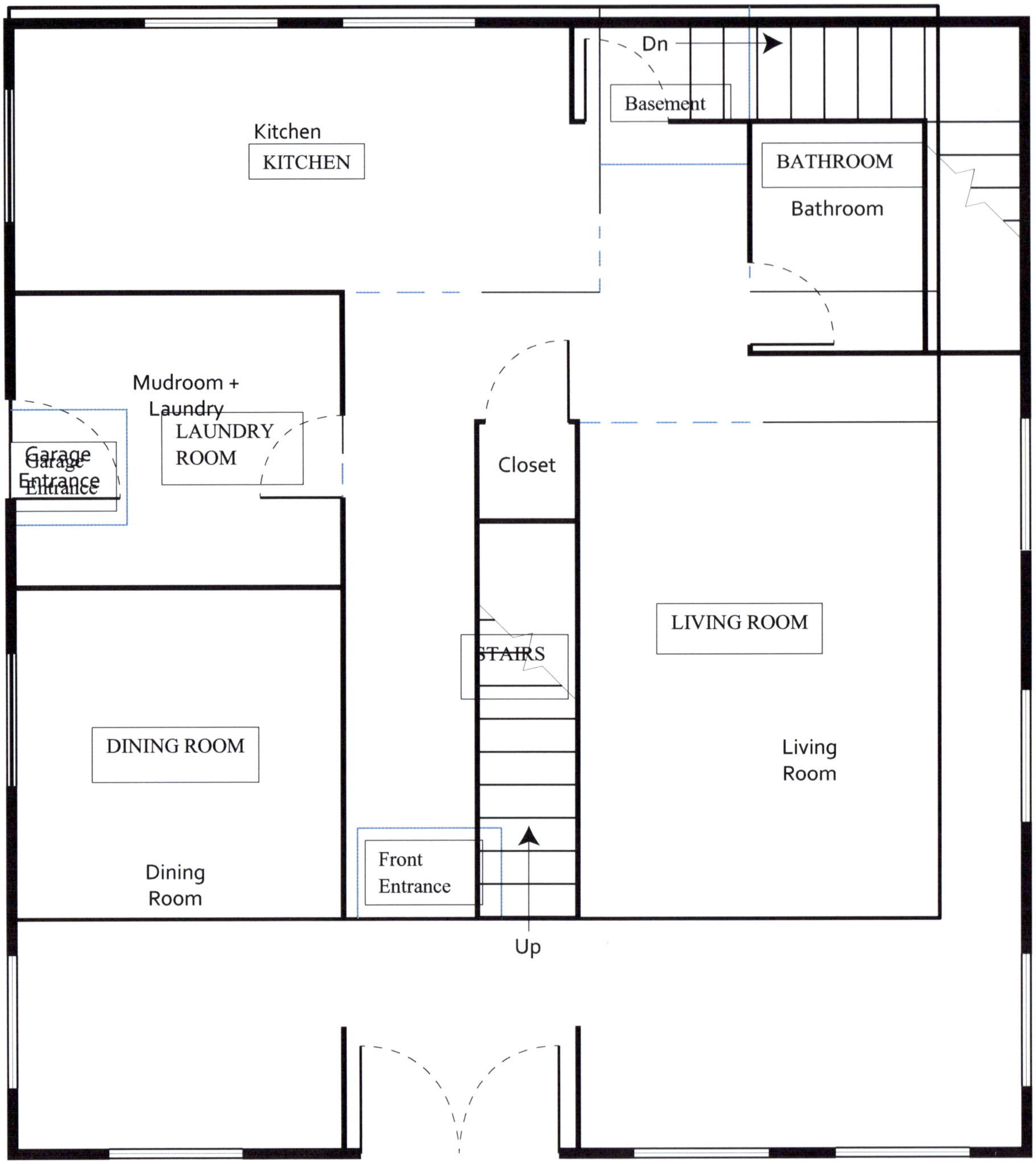
Dn
Basement
Kitchen
KITCHEN
BATHROOM
Bathroom
Mudroom +
Laundry
LAUNDRY
ROOM
Garage
Entrance
Closet
STAIRS
LIVING ROOM
DINING ROOM
Living
Room
Front
Entrance
Dining
Room
Up

STATEMENT OF: Name: Gary Fitzpeter DOB: 7/22/YEAR-34

Address: 8119 Calamity Way

Telephone No: 867-5309

I came home from a work trip at about 3 pm. Kids and Vonda said hello then took a nap while I put things away from work. Kids woke up and we ate dinner. Vonda began drinking, if she had not been already. She was drinking vodka & juice which is always trouble and did not eat. It was quickly evident that she was highly intoxicated. She was slurring her speech (could not say "cash" for example). She was also getting mean and rude as she does when she drinks way too much. I began to avoid her, hoping she would soon fall asleep. We quarreled a little bit about minor things and again I avoided her. Abbey lost one of her charms from her charms bracelet. I tried to help Vonda find it and she snapped at me. I said I was going downstairs to get away from her. I came back up a little later and the kitchen was destroyed. There were pots and pans everywhere. I fussed at her and she went off on me. I walked away again and she started to tell the kids what "a bastard" daddy is. I played with the kids alone in their room for about ½ hour. Then tried to get them wound down and ready for bed. She came from out of our room and said she was leaving, taking the kids to Ohio. She grabbed Abbey and I told her she was not driving anywhere that drunk, especially with the kids. She still headed to the car with Abbey and after she put her in the seat I grabbed her out and Vonda chased me back into the house. She was attacking me from behind. I got Abbey and Stan into the house and tried to talk to her in the garage away from the kids but she attacked me in the garage (kicks to the groin, punches, bit me on the shoulder). I fended her off repeatedly and she fell twice to the ground on the damp slick garage floor. The second time she fell was when she cut her head open. I did hold her down for a little bit to protect myself and keep her from driving intoxicated. I let her up when she promised not to drive drunk. As soon as I let her up, she ran out of the garage and started the car. When she left, I called 911.

* Note 1: I have lots of other documentation of previous incidents

* Note 2: She had taken my money, about $1000, and credit cards from my wallet.

* Note 3: Vonda has a lot of bruises on her arms and legs. She is probably going to say they came from me, but that is a lie. She plays Catcher for the lady Hellkats softball team. She had some games while I was out of town, and I'm pretty sure that's where the bruises came from. She is always getting bruised from softball games.

Signature: Gary Fitzpeter

GRANT OF IMMUNITY
IN THE MATTER OF

People of the State of Calamity	)	
v.	)	No. 123456
Vonda Fitzpeter	)	

GRANT OF IMMUNITY

To: Gary Fitzpeter:

1. It appears that you are a material witness for the government in the matter of *People of the State of Calamity v. Vonda Fitzpeter*; and

2. In consideration of your testimony as a witness for the government in the foregoing matter, you are hereby granted immunity from prosecution for any offense arising out of the matters therein involved concerning which you may be required to testify under oath; and

3. It is understood that this grant of immunity from prosecution is effective only upon the condition that you actually testify truthfully as a witness for the government. It is further understood that this grant of immunity from prosecution extends only to the offense or offenses that you were implicated in the matter herein set forth and concerning which you testify under oath.

M.J. JAVERT

M.J. Javert
State's Attorney

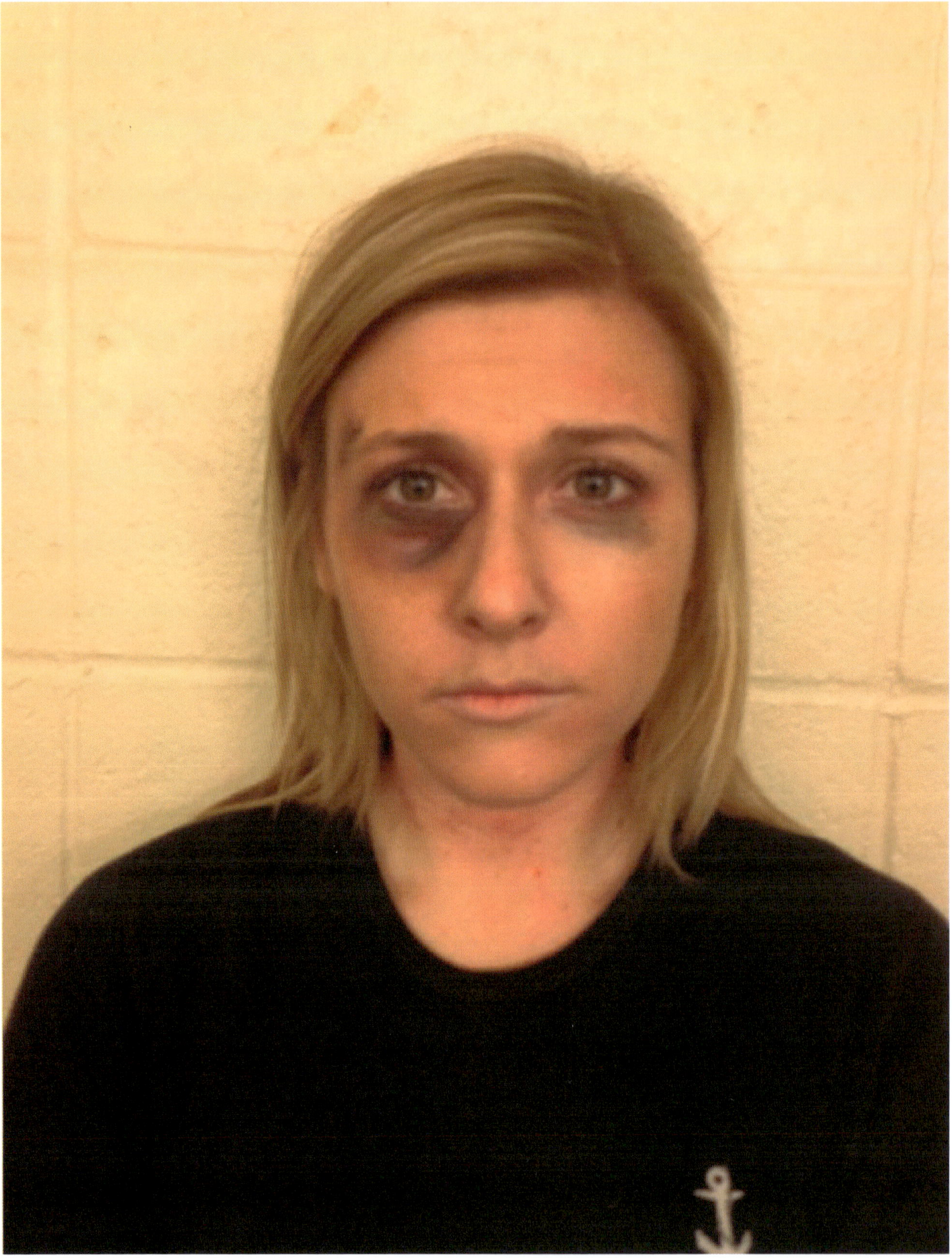

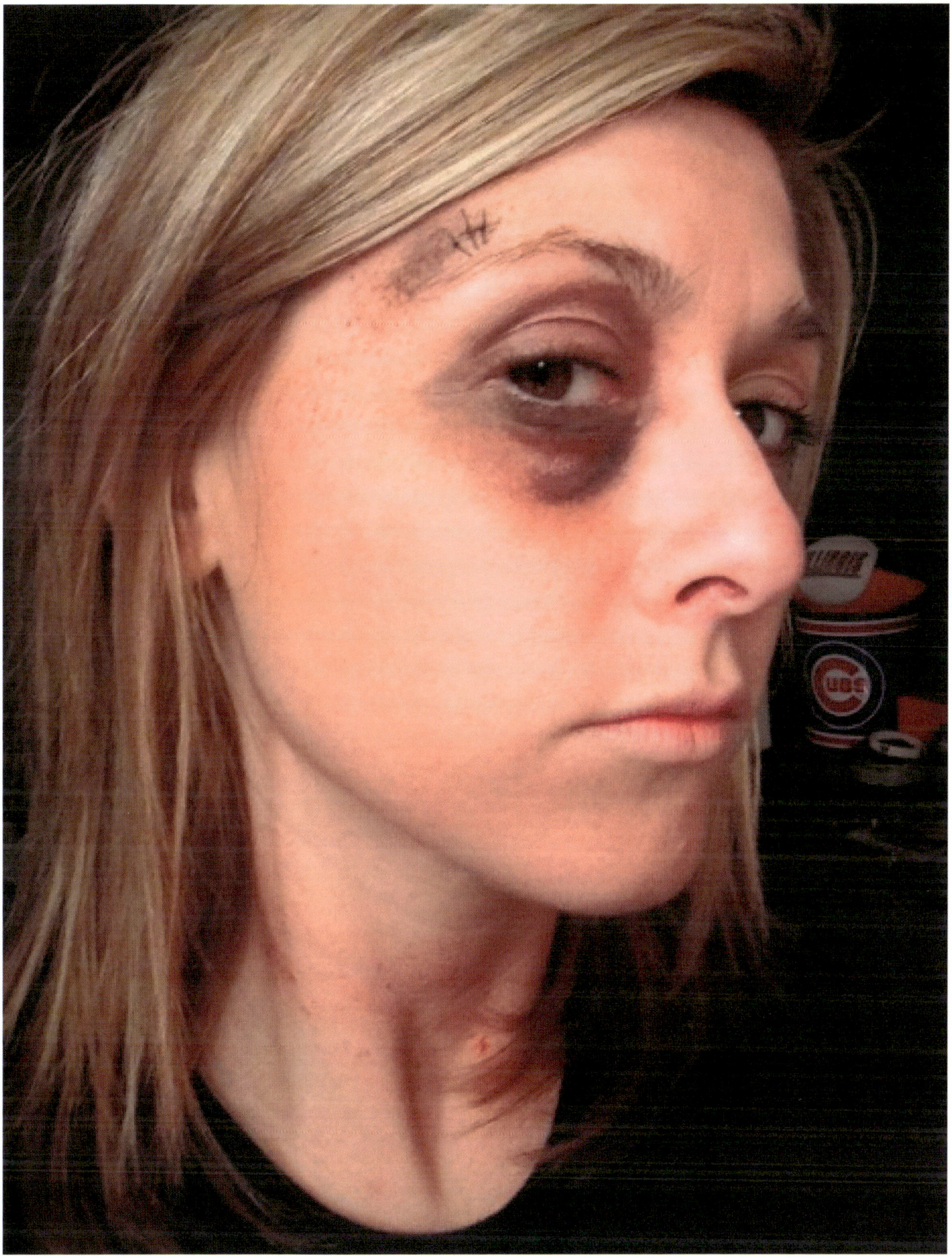
CUBS

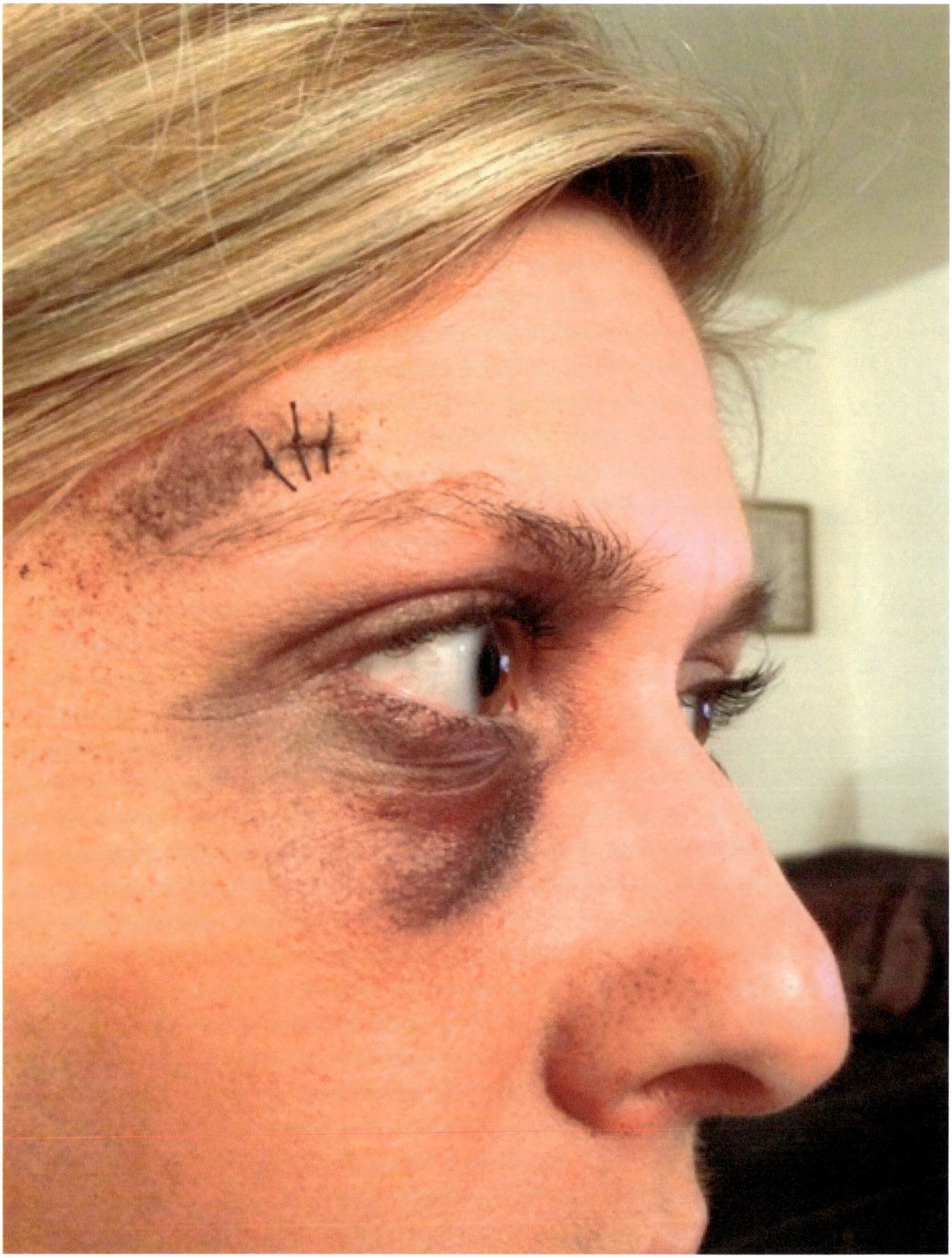

Main
Pine
Fremont
513 Fremont
Elm St
Willow St
Mobile Dr
Carney Dr
Oakwood Cemetery
LilyWhite. designs
Oakwood Dr
Oakwood Ct
West Oak
Drive 6 min
2.0 mi
Crab Orchard Golf Club
Route Traveled by
Vonda Fitzpeter
West Oak
Country Club
S Greenbriar Rd
Jeffrey Dr
Cheryl Dr
Lynne Ln
Mockingbird Ln
Partridge
Calamity Way
8119
Mockingbird
Breeze Dr
Sunrise Dr

CALAMITY CITY FIRE DEPT. EMS
500 N. MAIN ST., CALAMITY CITY, CALAMITY, 66666

Tuesday, July 10, YEAR-1

<table>
<tr><td colspan="2">
<u>Patient</u>

Name: Fitzpeter, Vonda
Race/Sex: White/Female
DOB/Age: 03/28/YEAR-33 / 33

Address: 8119 Calamity Way
City: Calamity City
State: Calamity Zip: 66666

Phone: 867-5309

P MD: Litzer, M.
</td></tr>
<tr><td colspan="2">
<u>Run Information</u> (7/10/ YEAR-1)

Run # 1: 1200000891 Run # 3:
Run # 2: Run # 4:

Scene: 513 Fremont St.
City: Calamity City
State: Calamity Zip: 66666

Driver: Jarvis, Wayne
Att 1: Danish, Rae Att 3:
Att 2: Holt, Stew Att 4:
Veh. ID: 3S09
Place: In City Type: 911 Response (Scene)

Reported By: Danish Level: ALS, Level 1 Emergency
</td></tr>
<tr><td>
<u>Type of Run</u>

To Scene: Non Emergency No Lights or Sirens
From Scene: Treat/Transport
<u>Units on Scene</u>

Local Law Enforcement – Calamity City PD
</td><td>
<u>Call Times</u>
Received: 21:05:00
Dispatched: 21:06:00
En Route: 21:07:00
Arrive Loc: 21:09:09
Depart Loc: 21:30:01
Arrive Dest: 21:43:00
In Service: 22:25:00
</td></tr>
<tr><td colspan="2">
<u>Primary Assessment</u>

IOC – Conscious
Airway – Patent
Chest – Equal Expansion
Breath – Clear
Skin – Normal Color/Normal Moisture/Normal Temp
</td></tr>
</table>

CapRefill - <2 RPupil – AK LPupil – AK
<u>Chronological</u> VONDA FITZPETER is a 33 yr old White female with a primary complaint of Assault. Dispatched as… Assault. Initial Observed Condition… Conscious Patient History: Anxiety / Depression Patient Allergies: None Patient Medications: Xanex Prozac Primary Assessment: Airway – Patent Chest – Equal Expansion Breath – Clear/Equal Skin – Normal Color/Normal Moisture/Normal Temp CapRefill - <2 RPupil – AK/No reaction to Light LPupil – AK/No reaction to Light Patient GCS = 15 (Eye = 4; Verbal = 5; Motor = 6) Illness Assessment: Trauma Assessment: Right Eye = Laceration/Pain/Swelling/Tenderness Nose = Pain/Swelling Right Humerus = Bruise Neck: Redness and possible brusing. All Else = Negative Patient RTS = 12 (BP = 4; Resp = 4; GCS = 15) Stretcher Used <Non Aumbulatory> Moved VIA <Long Back Board> The following actions were performed: Bleeding Controlled by Danish EKG Monitor by Holt Glucose Test by Holt IV Therapy by Danish IV Peripheral by Danish Oxygen by Holt Other BLS by Jarvis Spinal Immobilization by Holt

Other ALS by Danish
The following Invasive Procedures were performed:
<<Assessment – Adult>> by Danish – At 21:10:00
<<Cervical collar application>> by Jarvis – At 21:19:00
<<Spinal Immobilization>> by Holt – At 21:20:00
<<Transported on stretcher secured with belts>> by Danish – At 21:21:00
<<Patient Loaded>> by Danish – At 21:23:00

<<Intravenous established>> /Prepared equipment/Explain procedure to patient/Applied tourniquet/Palpitated vein/Prepared site with antiseptic solution/Punctured vein/Advanced catheter into vein/Removed needle and discarded into biohazard sharps container/Connected IV tubing/Removed antibacterial and cover to site/Secured catheter and tubing in place by Danish – At 21:26:00
<<Pulse Oximetry>> by Danish – At 21:26:00
<<Intravenous electrolyte solutions Sodium Chloride>> by Danish – At 21:27:00
<<ECG – 3 lead>> by Holt – At 21:28:00
<<Blood Glucose Analysis>> /Followed BSI precautions/Test Strips not expired/Test Strip inserted correctly into machine/3-Digit code that appeared on screen matched code on strip vial/Utilized IV catheter blood/Window on Test Strip completely filled with blood/Removed strip and discarded in biohazard container/Placed dressing over the puncture site/Documented B/S/ reading by Holt – At 21:28:00
<<Contact Medical Control>> by Holt – At 21:33:00
<<Patient Off-Loaded>> by Weathers – At 21:44:00

Protective Equip: None

Time	Position	Blood Pressure	Pulse	Resp	SAO2
21:24:00	R Lay	122/90	125	20	98

Time	Intervention	Size	Route	Dosage	Volume
21:10:00	Assessment - Adult				
21:19:00	Cervical collar application				
21:20:00	Spinal immobilization				
21:21:00	Transported on stretcher				
21:23:00	Patient loaded				
21:26:00	Intravenous established	20	L Antecu.		
21:26:00	Pulse Oximetry				98
21:27:00	Intravenous electrolyte				
	Solutions Sodium Chloride		IV	tko	50cc
21:27:00	ECG – 3 Lead				
21:28:00	Oxygen		Nasal	4lpm	
21:28:00	Blood glucose analysis				112
21:33:00	Contact Medical Control				
21:44:00	Patient Off-Loaded				

CALAMITY CITY E.R.

Name	First	Middle	Last
	Vonda		Fitzpeter

Sex	Age	Date of Admission	Time of Admission	Date of Discharge	Time of Discharge
Female	33	7/10/YEAR-1	21:43	7/10/YEAR-1	23:00

Address Street	City	State	Zip
8119 Calamity Way	Calamity City	Calamity	66666

Telephone Number	Brought in by
867-5309	Officer Pat Pelfrey

Vital Signs	Examining Physician	Nurse's Initials
B.P. 120/80	T. Fishman, MD	L.A.

☐ X-Ray ☐ EKG ☐ Lab ☐ Pharm ☐ M&S

Allergies:

History:

Exam:
Patient was intoxicated upon arrival with a BAC of .17 as reported by police. She suffered a laceration above her right eye that was accompanied by some minor swelling.

Treatment:
Treated the laceration and patient was discharged in police custody

Calamity County State's Attorney
Investigative Services
2323 Courthouse Road
Calamity City, Calamity 66666

October 30, YEAR-1

Mary Jane Calamity
Calamity County State's Attorney
2323 Courthouse Road
Calamity City, Calamity 66666

Re: Report of Investigation into July 10 Arrest of Vonda Fitzpeter

Dear Ms. Calamity,

Pursuant to your request, this office has conducted a background investigation into the potential defense witnesses in the case of *People v. Vonda Fitzpeter*. The results of that investigation are below.

1. Vonda Fitzpeter

No prior arrests or convictions in State of Calamity. A DUI 11 years ago in Freebridge, Ohio. BAC for DUI was .10. Fitzpeter pled guilty to misdemeanor DUI and paid a fine.

On September 10, YEAR-1, the undersigned interviewed neighbors of the defendant, Vonda Fitzpeter. None were willing to go on record, but consensus was that she is a nice person when sober, and temperamental when intoxicated. Neighbors on either side of home reported hearing her yelling profanities at children and husband on weekends. Neighbors also reported hearing Gary Fitzpeter's voice raised in anger. One neighbor said he was surprised no one had ever called the police prior to July 10.

The undersigned learned from neighbors that Vonda Fitzpeter plays catcher for the Marko's Bar and Grill Lady Hellkats Softball Team in the Calamity City Chamber of Commerce Women's Fastpitch Softball League. The undersigned spoke to the coach of the team, Laura Lamper. Lamper spoke highly of Fitzpeter and said she was a "great catcher when sober." Lamper said Vonda had a drinking problem and she had talked to her a couple of times about letting up on the alcohol for the good of the team. She thought Vonda responded well to it. Lamper said Vonda was the kind of player who would sacrifice her body to make a play and commented that she was always getting bruised up in games, usually on her arms and legs. Lamper was unaware of any domestic violence with Vonda specifically but said it was a problem on the team and that many women were victims of abusive spouses or partners. She said she had met Gary Fitzpeter at a couple of games. In her opinion, he was "a real asshole." She had to kick him out of the dugout one game when he came in and started berating Vonda for striking out with the bases loaded and two outs. He also would bring Vonda's son into the dugout so Vonda could change his diaper. She said it wouldn't surprise her if there were abuse situations in that home.

Fitzpeter has not worked since moving to Calamity City. This office was unable to receive funds to travel to Freebridge, Ohio, her former city of residence to visit or interview former employers.

2. Tiffany Clarke

No prior arrests or convictions.

Clarke is currently unemployed. The undersigned interviewed Clarke on September 12, YEAR-1 and obtained her prior employment history. Clarke worked in the makeup department of Federated Department Store in the River's Edge Mall. She worked there from January 10, YEAR-6 to June 15, YEAR-1. She told the undersigned that she resigned voluntarily to spend more time with her children.

The undersigned went to the Human Resources Department at Federated on September 12, YEAR-1 and interviewed the Human Resources manager. Ms. Clarke was terminated for cause for misusing her employee discount to buy clothing and makeup for people outside her immediate family. She initially lied to store investigators about it, but when confronted with security video, told the truth. The company agreed not to press charges if she made restitution of $78.36.

3. Stanley Jones, Jr.

No arrests or prior convictions.

The undersigned called Jones on 13 September YEAR-1 and obtained employment history. Jones has worked for Local 3124 of the International Brotherhood of Pipefitters since 1970. The undersigned called Local 3124 and verified the employment history. The union official commented that Jones was "exemplary" and "spotless." Jones said he did not have much to say other than he knew Gary was trouble from the beginning and he always knew Gary would hurt Vonda. He said he already gave a statement and didn't want to talk about it anymore. He said the Calamity State's Attorney was "evil" for prosecuting Vonda.

The undersigned called Marvin Fitzpeter, the father of Gary Fitzpeter, on 13 September YEAR-1, to ask about his relationship with Jones. Marvin was eager to talk. According to Marvin, Jones was president of the Freebridge High School Athletic Booster Club the year that Gary Fitzpeter was a senior. Marvin said that Jones loved Gary "like a son" until Gary was ejected from the quarterfinal game after striking a referee. Jones always blamed Gary for the team losing the game. At the time the team lost, they were ranked #1 in the state and, with 5 Division I football prospects on the team, were heavily favored to win the game. Marvin said that Gary was a great football player but "a little hotheaded in a competition environment." Gary was being recruited by several Division I programs, including Ohio State, Kent State, Akron, and Marshall. After the game, Jones called every one of the coaches to tell them what had happened and "basically blacklisted Gary." Gary lost all his scholarship offers and ended up never going to college.

Marvin said that he and Jones had been good friends until this incident, but since then, their relationship was frosty at best. "You don't get along with people who attack your kids," he explained. He said it was especially difficult when Gary and Vonda started dating. "I told her to stay away from her," he said, noting that Vonda had substance abuse problems and had been in "lots of shack-up relationships with guys." But he said Gary loved her and thought it would be different with her. He said Gary had changed since the marriage and was always stressed and anxious. Marvin felt that Vonda was physically abusive towards Gary and would strike or hit him, relying on the size differential and Gary's "restraint" to avoid retaliation. Gary had told Marvin that Vonda drank heavily and he was worried she was an alcoholic, but she wouldn't get help.

Marvin felt Jones would say anything to hurt Gary and said, "at some point you have to get over a high school football game, and he just can't." He said that Jones and Vonda had always had a "terrible" relationship and thought his indifference towards her was the cause of her drinking and substance abuse. "It would've been a lot different if she could run a 4.5 40 and play running back," he said. "All he cared about was his son, Stanley the Third."

When the undersigned asked Marvin about the incident between Gary and Mindy Ferguson, Marvin said there was "a huge misunderstanding there, and I'm not going to talk about it." He said it was interesting that Jones had mentioned that situation, given that Stanley the Third and Mindy had dated most of high school and lived together for a year after Stanley the Third graduated from college. "I could tell you some stories about STIII," he said. "But I won't."

4. <u>Lee Austera</u>

Arrested in 1992 for disturbing the peace at a Greenpeace demonstration in Puget Sound, Washington. Charges dropped.

Arrested in 1996 for trespassing on a federal nuclear facility during a demonstration at the Paducah Gaseous Diffusion nuclear processing plant in Paducah, Kentucky. Charges dropped.

Arrested in YEAR-10 for damaging a government vehicle during a "Stop Police Brutality" demonstration at the Calamity Highway Patrol headquarters in Calamity City. Charges dropped.

No convictions.

Has worked at the Calamity Hospital since 1997. Member of the Board of Directors of the Calamity Women's Shelter. Refused to talk to the undersigned when I visited the hospital on 14 September YEAR-1. A co-worker, on condition of anonymity, briefly spoke to undersigned and explained that Austera is strongly anti-police and believes most police organizations are instruments of official brutality. "Everyone knows he/she hates the cops," she said. "He/She gets upset whenever a police officer is here. Really upset."

CALAMITY CITY POLICE DEPARTMENT – CASE NO. 11-11-11 DATE 7/12/YEAR-1

STATEMENT OF: Name: Vonda Fitzpeter DOB: 11/11/Year-33

Address: Calamity City Women's Shelter, 1234 Waverly Way

Telephone No: 867-5309

Gary had been away from home for the week on a business trip. It was nice to have him gone because he is angry and moody most of the time. When he is home, he is always complaining about my housekeeping, my cooking, my weight, and the way I raise the kids. I am a fun mom and would rather have a good day playing with the kids than a spotless house.

He got home on Sunday afternoon. He was upset when he came home because the house was messy. There were toys everywhere and several baskets of laundry I hadn't gotten around to folding yet. But the kids and I had a great weekend. We went to a birthday party, and played at the park. They had some friends over. The house was cluttered but not dirty. I tried to tell him that but he got upset. He asked what we were having for dinner and I told him frozen lasagna and it would be ready at about 5 or 6. I had put it in the oven when I heard his truck in the driveway. He said something like, "That figures. Gone for a week and I come home to a filthy house, a drunk wife, and a f-ing TV dinner. Welcome home, Gary. Now go screw yourself." He can be pretty sarcastic and mean when he's mad.

I did have a couple of drinks while I was waiting for him to come home. Some vodka and orange juice. I ate a bowl of cereal for breakfast with the kids but I didn't have lunch. I usually skip lunch because I am trying to watch my weight. I probably had two or three drinks. Not too many. But enough to feel kind of a buzz and help me get through him coming home. I should have had something to eat. I know it isn't a good idea to drink on an empty stomach, especially for someone my size. I'm kind of a lightweight when it comes to alcohol. The police told me my BAC when they arrested me was .17 but I don't believe it. I didn't have that much to drink. I was buzzed, but I was able to think straight and drive my car without any problems. No way was I a .17. I don't think I was even at a .10 if you want to know the truth.

I want to point out that Officer Taylor and Gary are good friends and go hunting together several times a year. They went to high school together and have been drinking buddies for about 15 years. Officer Pelfrey's brother Hank works with Gary, and Officer Pelfrey has also gone hunting with Gary several times, along with Hank. Gary has their numbers in his cellphone. They also play poker together and take turns hosting the game. When it's at our house, I cook for everyone and do what I can to make sure it's a fun night for them. They've been to our house lots of times. I think Gary actually called Taylor or Pelfrey directly when I left the house instead of calling 911. Taylor met me IN Tiffany's driveway, and the only way he would have known I was going there was if Gary told him. I would not be surprised if Officer Taylor did something to the BAC readout or record to make things look worse. They seized some bottles of alcohol from my car. I told them I thought Gary probably planted them there and I asked them to check them for fingerprints. Instead, I've been told the Calamity PD destroyed the bottles without testing them for fingerprints or DNA or anything like that. I asked them two or three times to test them right after they arrested me. I know for a fact I told them Gary had to have planted them there. I would never put open containers of alcohol in my car.

When Gary got home, he poured a drink for himself. I think it was Wild Turkey. We have a lot of alcohol in the house. We both like to drink, but Gary has a real problem with it. Most nights he goes to bed drunk. Usually beer but sometimes hard alcohol. He was already being a real jerk, and I knew it would be worse once he started drinking, so I told him I was going to take a nap. I went in the kids' room with them and they played while I took a nap. I could hear Gary stomping in and out of the garage putting his things away and swearing about how the kids had gotten into his fishing poles and nets.

I woke up from my nap at about 5 or a little later. The bedroom door was open and the kids had left the room. I could hear Abbey crying downstairs. She was in the living room. Gary was watching some kind of sports show on TV and drinking a beer. There was a dirty plate and a fork on the floor that looked like he had eaten lasagna. He was holding Stan, our 2-year-old, on his lap. They are pretty close. I have to say, Gary is a good Dad to Stan. He really is. Gary was ignoring Abbey, which is pretty typical for him. She isn't his daughter. She is mine from a previous relationship. Gary has always refused to consider adopting her, even though her father doesn't want anything to do with her and won't pay child support or visit her. She was upset that she lost a charm from the bracelet that my mom gave her for her birthday. She said it had fallen off in the kitchen. So I went to the kitchen with her to look for it. Gary had taken the lasagna out of the oven and cut a piece of it for himself. It was on top of the stove. We pulled the refrigerator out and took the drawer from under the oven. There was a lot of dirt and dust under both the oven and the fridge, so I started cleaning it up. I had the broom out, and there were some pots and pans on the floor too. I was looking through the dirt for the charm from the bracelet when Gary come upstairs to get some more lasagna. He blew up when he saw the kitchen. He called me a bunch of names, including a bitch and a whore. He said I was a drunk slob. And he kicked me. I was sitting on the floor sifting through a pile of dirt I'd swept up from under the oven and looking for that charm from Abbey's bracelet.

He kicked me in the ribs. Really hard. And he pulled my hair and said "You bitch you had better get this whole house cleaned or you will get what's coming to you." He was angry. Really angry. My head hurt from him pulling my hair, and I started to cry. That made him even angrier and he called me some more names, and he kicked me again. Gary has been violent with me before. Nothing real major. Nothing that I went to the hospital for or anything, but he's grabbed my arms and held me, hit me, pulled my hair. I still had some bruises from the last time, the day before he went on his business trip. I've slapped him a couple of times in the past, and scratched him. But he's a big guy, about six three and two hundred and fifty pounds. I'm about five two, one thirty. I couldn't hurt him if I tried.

So Abbey saw Gary pulling my hair and kicking me, and she started crying. Don't do it, she said. Don't do it. He let go of my hair and threw me down on the ground. Abbey covered me up with her body, and he laughed and walked away.

I hugged Abbey. I think I told her that Daddy Gary (that's what we call him) was a real bastard. I'm pretty sure he could hear it, because he yelled that I should shut up if I knew what was good for me. I decided to take the kids and leave Gary. I was going to go to my friend Tiffany's house and calm down, then drive the next day to my parents' house in Ohio. I texted her and she texted back and said I could come over.

I took Abbey to her room, and I went out to the garage to get some suitcases. Gary followed me out there and asked what I was doing. I told him I was going to leave him and take the kids to Ohio to my parents. He told me I was crazy and drunk and he would make sure I never made it out of Calamity City, let alone Ohio. He reminded me that he was friends with half the police force and he said he could fix it so I would go to jail and lose the kids. He said I was an unfit mother.

He grabbed one of the suitcases from me, but I was able to keep hold of the big one, and I made it back into the house. I started throwing things into the suitcase. My clothes and some clothes for the kids. I heard Gary in the kitchen, getting into the fridge or freezer. I think he took out a bottle of vodka from the freezer, and he must have put it in my car while I was packing.

I got the suitcase packed, and then I went into my closet. I have a small purse in there that Gary doesn't know about. My Dad doesn't like Gary, he knows he is abusive because he and my Mom have seen the bruises and heard some of the things Gary has said. My Dad gave me $1,000 in cash a couple of years ago in case I ever needed to get away. I had to promise I wouldn't use it for anything else. So I got the money and put it into my bra. Then I saw Gary's wallet on the dresser, and I took out his credit cards and whatever cash he had. I didn't count it. It was a bunch of 20's and 5's. We don't have joint accounts—he controls all the money—and I don't have my own credit card. I have to ask him when I need to use one. So I put his credit cards in my bra too, and I put his wallet back on the dresser.

I got the suitcase, then I picked up Stan from the living room, and I grabbed Abbey's hand. We headed for the garage, but Gary got in front of the door and blocked my way. "You aren't going anywhere," he said. "You're too drunk. And you aren't taking the kids anywhere. Not even Abbey." I could smell alcohol on his breath, and I knew he was drunk. His eyes were bloodshot. Later, when the police arrested me, I asked them to test his blood alcohol, but I don't think they ever did.

I told him I had only had a couple of drinks and I needed to get out of there with the kids. I told him we could talk about all this later after we both had the chance to cool down and he sobered up. Then I tried to push past him.

He grabbed Stan from me and held him up where I couldn't reach him. I let go of Abbey's hand and pushed him in the chest. I figured if I could get the door open, he'd know I was serious and let me have Stan back. As I was pushing past him, he kicked me from behind, right into the door. I tripped and hit the door with my face. Right on my nose.

He put Stan down in the office right next to the door. Meanwhile, I opened the garage door to get out. I had let go of the suitcase, but I grabbed Abbey and pulled her into the garage. He came out the door and shoved me into the wall and said I wasn't going anywhere.

I punched him in the chest as hard as I could. And I clawed his arm to get him to move. And that's when he started choking me and beating on me. He threw me down by my neck onto the concrete floor. I hit my head and started bleeding. He slammed my head into the floor a couple of times. And he held me down and choked me. Abbey was screaming that he was going to kill me.

I thought I was going to black out. I started gagging from getting choked. I looked up and saw Stan coming out the door. Gary got off me to get Stan, and I got up and ran out of the garage. I was able to get into my car and drive away. I figured I would go to Tiffany's where I could be safe and maybe she and her boyfriend could come get Abbey and Stan for me.

Tiffany lives about a mile and a half away. As I turned on to her street, there was a police car right behind me and another one turning into her driveway. The car behind me put on its lights and I pulled over and got arrested for DUI.

I can't remember which officer pulled me over. I was pretty upset. But I saw the alcohol bottles, and I told them about how Gary planted them and that they should check them for fingerprints. I told them Gary had beaten me and I had to get away from him.

After one of the officers put me against his car, I saw Abbey get out of the back seat. I was shocked. I had no idea she was even in there. I tried to run over and hug her and ask her how she got in the car, but the officer wouldn't let me. I saw the other police officer put Abbey into his car and drive away. I asked where Abbey was being taken, and the officer told me she was going back to Gary. This made me even more upset. I wasn't sure what Gary would do to her once Abbey got back home.

They called an ambulance, and the paramedics took me to the emergency room. I got some treatment there for the laceration on my face and the bruising. I have bruises on my arms and my body where he kicked me, and on my neck where he choked me. They had to do X-rays and everything to make sure I didn't have a fractured skull. They put me in a hospital gown—one of the ones with no back—

and when I got released from the ER, Officer Pelfrey picked me up and walked me in handcuffs past everyone in the ER and into the car. I was humiliated. He treated me like a common criminal.

I stayed the night at Tiffany's, and the next morning I went to the women's shelter, where I am now staying. They took me to a judge and I got an order of protection against Gary. I also got custody of the kids, but he gave them to his mother in Kentucky. She came up and got them. I know the police talked to Abbey and I am sure Gary told her what to say about me falling down on my own. It isn't true. He kicked me and pushed me down. But I don't blame Abbey. She's only six and I know she was afraid for my life.

I hope the sheriff is able to find my kids soon. I miss them.

Signature: Vonda Fitzpeter

CALAMITY CITY POLICE DEPARTMENT – CASE NO.11-11-11 DATE 7/13/YEAR-1

STATEMENT OF: Name: *Tiffany Clarke* DOB: 7/22/Year-32

Address: *513 Fremont Street, Calamity City, Calamity*

Telephone No: *867-9284*

My best friend is Vonda Fitzpeter. I have come to the police station to provide information about the events that happened on Sunday the 11th. The police did not interview me at the time they arrested Vonda for DUI, even though it was in my driveway. We have been friends for three years now, ever since she moved to Calamity City with Gary. He's her husband now, but they were just living together then. Once she found out she was pregnant with Stan, they got married. Which I think was a big mistake. She is a very good friend to me, even closer than my sister or my Mom. We watch each other's kids all the time and spend a lot of time together. We have everything in common, from music to kids to experiences we've had. We talk and text on the phone every day and see each other almost every day.

She and Gary have a bad marriage. He's a jerk and doesn't appreciate what he has in her. And he's controlling about everything. They don't have any joint accounts. She has to ask him for money all the time. And he's critical of her. He calls her names. He's always on her about her weight. Which is just fine, by the way. I wish I looked as good as her. Whenever we go out together, guys are always hitting on her. She just shows them her ring and they walk away. She could do a lot better than Gary, that's for sure. He's a real jerk, and he has problems with alcohol. On top of that, he's a mean drunk. When he gets drunk, he becomes abusive. Sometimes he hits her. I've even seen him hit her a couple of times. She has also slapped him and scratched him a couple of times, but he had it coming, if you ask me.

She's stayed at my house five or six times in YEAR-1 or so. He's given her black eyes, bruises, a bloody nose, and he's pulled some of her hair out before. I keep trying to get her to call the police on him and get a restraining order, but she won't do it. He makes pretty good money, he's in some kind of sales, and I think she is afraid of losing that. But she'd be better off without him.

On Sunday the 11th, it was a pretty stressful day for her. Gary had been off on a business trip and he was coming home. And she hadn't cleaned the house or anything. She's not the best housekeeper, and she hadn't done anything all week while he was gone. She'd had a couple of softball games. I brought my kids to watch her. She plays catcher, and she's pretty good.

I'd been there Saturday night with my kids, and they made a real mess. Toys everywhere. Dishes and food in the kitchen. I was going to stay and help her clean up, but the kids were tired and we'd both been drinking and were pretty tired. She said she'd get it taken care of the next day. She called me in the morning and told me she just couldn't get it all done and it was overwhelming. Her speech was a little slurred, but she could've just been tired. She asked if I could come help, but I couldn't because one of my kid's fathers was in town and he had supervised visitation at my house, so I couldn't go anywhere. I told her to make a list and start with one thing at a time. She said she'd start with a drink and we both laughed. I said I would too.

It was probably 10 in the morning when we talked. I didn't hear from her again until later in the day. I think it was around six or so. Could have been later. I wasn't tracking it. She sent me a text message. It said, "He just kicked me and pulled my hair. Abbey screaming. Can I bring kids over and stay with U 2-nite? Going to Mom and Dad's tomorrow." I texted back. "Sure. Need any help over there?" She never replied to that text.

Maybe a hour or so later I heard from her again. This time it was a phone call from her cell phone. She sounded really bad. She was kind of wailing and crying and I had to keep telling her to calm down. It was really hard to understand what she was saying at first because of the way she was wailing and screaming. She said, "He just tried to kill me! He smashed my head into the floor and choked me! He was killing me! In front of the kids!" I didn't ask who she was talking about because I knew it was Gary. I told her to calm down and I would call the police and come over and get her. She said she was in her car on the way to my house. I asked her where the kids were and she started wailing again and said "He's got them! He wouldn't give them to me!"

I went out the front door to look for her. I don't live that far away, maybe a mile and a half or so. I was going to call the police, but right after I walked outside, a police car pulled into my driveway. I started to walk over to it, and then I saw Vonda's car turn onto the street. There was a police car right behind her with its lights on.

She pulled over right before my driveway and got out of the car. There was blood all over her face, her hair, and her blouse. She had on a light-colored yellow blouse and it was just drenched in blood. She had a big gash over one of her eyes. I was going to go give her a hug, but the police grabbed her instead and took her over to the police car with its lights on.

She was screaming and crying, "He tried to kill me! He tried to kill me! He's got my babies!" I've never seen her that upset before. And like I said, there was blood everywhere. They wouldn't let me talk to her.

While the police were talking to her, the back door of the car opened and her six-year-old daughter Abbey Jones came out. I ran over to Abbey and hugged her and asked how she was doing. Vonda seemed really surprised that Abbey was in the car and she said, "I thought Daddy wouldn't let you come with me!" I asked Abbey what happened and she told me that Gary had kicked Vonda, pulled her hair, choked her and slammed her head into the floor. She also said that Vonda had punched and scratched Gary. She said Gary was really mean when he came home.

We didn't get long to talk before one of the police officers came over and separated Abbey from me.

About ten minutes later, an ambulance showed up, and a couple of paramedics put her in it and drove off. I was able to walk over to the door and I told her I loved her. She asked me to go get her baby from Gary. She meant her little one, Stan.

I went into the house. My child's father, Ronnie, was still there on his supervised visitation. I told him I was going to have to help out a friend for a little while and could he watch the kids for a couple of minutes. I told him I needed to trust him, and he said he would do it.

So I got in the car and drove over to Vonda's. A police car was in the driveway, and an officer was standing in the garage talking to Gary. I got out and walked up to the officer. I told him I was Vonda's best friend and I was there to get the kids. The officer told me I needed to leave and it would all get sorted out. So I left. There wasn't anything I could do. I did see Abbey looking out the window, and I waved at her when I left. I've heard that Gary got Abbey to tell the police that he didn't do anything to Vonda and she fell down on her own. That's just the kind of thing he would do, trying to manipulate a child like that.

Later that night—I think it was a little before midnight-the police brought Vonda over to my house. She was still pretty shaken up. She acted woozy, but I think it was from her head injury and not alcohol. I made a bed for her on the couch, and the next morning I took her to the women's shelter. Then I went with her to the courthouse and she got a order of protection against Gary and custody of the kids. But it was too late to get the kids. His mom had come up from Kentucky and gotten them. Later in the afternoon, we went to the house to get her things with a police officer. Everything was clean.

When we went through the garage, she showed me where he had hit her head on the floor. There was still a couple of drops of blood on the floor, but it looked like the floor, the freezer, and the wall had all been scrubbed clean.

I think it's wrong that she has gotten charged with DUI and domestic battery when she is the one who nearly got killed. And I also think it is wrong that Gary's Mom has those kids. Vonda is pretty upset about what Gary did to her, but she is even more upset that she doesn't have her kids with her. And I don't blame her.

And I want to say something else about this case, too. My brother's girlfriend, Mindy Dassity, is a waitress at the Fryin Pan Café downtown. Most of the cops and firemen go there for breaks. She told me she was serving a couple of police officers a few days before this happened, and she overheard them talking about Gary and Vonda. One of them said, "She's a looker, but it's too bad for Gary she's such a drunk." And the other one said, "Well, she'll get what's coming to her." Mindy said those same officers came in the day after all this happened and she heard one of them say, "I told you she'd get what was coming to her. I hope she likes it in jail." Mindy said one of the officers was Officer Pelfrey. She didn't know who the other officer was.

I think someone should charge Gary with attempted murder and kidnapping.

Signature: *Tiffany Clarke*

STATEMENT OF: Name: Stanley Jones, Jr. DOB: 8/01/Year-63

Address: 4321 Forthright Lane, Freebridge, Ohio

Telephone No: 234-5678

I, Stanley Jones, Jr., of Freebridge, Ohio, have come voluntarily and of my own free will and choice to the Calamity City Police Department to make a statement in the case involving my daughter, Vonda and her husband Gary. By trade I am a union pipefitter and have been in the union since Year-44, when I graduated from high school. I work on power plant retrofits. When a power company takes a plant offline, my crews and I will come in and remove and re-install high-pressure steam pipes. We do coal-fired, natural gas, nuclear.

My wife Cheryl and I have two children. Our oldest, Stanley Jones, III, is a police officer in Cleveland. Major crimes detective. He has been on the force for about 20 years now. He was always a great kid. All-state linebacker on the football team and played for the Kent State Golden Flashes while he was getting his criminal justice degree. Cheryl and I never missed a game. Home or away. Pee Wee Football through College. He earned a starting job hallway through his freshman year and never lost it. He wasn't big enough to play in the NFL, but he had the heart. I wish he would have done it.

He and his wife have three beautiful little daughters. We'd like them to try again and see if they can get a grandson for us so we can watch another Jones play football in a few years, but I don't think they're going to do it. She's an aerobics instructor and she's a little vain about her appearance. Give her credit, though. She has reason to be.

Vonda is our youngest. She was always a lot more rebellious than ST III—that's what everyone calls my son—but she has a good heart. The biggest problem she ever had in her life was falling in love with Gary Fitzpeter. Gary was on the football team in high school with Stan. Even back in high school, he had a reputation of being a violent jerk. He got kicked out of three games his senior year for fighting. Including the quarterfinals of the state playoffs. He played defensive end, and he got a roughing the quarterback penalty for throwing the guy down by the neck and slamming his head into the turf. When the ref threw the penalty flag, he punched the ref and got kicked out of the game. It was an away game, and he got escorted off the field by two state troopers and held on the team bus until the end of the game. Up until he got that penalty, we were ahead by two points, but that penalty put the other team in scoring position and they ended up winning the game on a field goal by one point. Everyone knew Gary cost us the game, and Gary knew it too.

He already had problems with drinking and drugs. Everyone on the team covered for him because he was so talented—Ohio State offered him a preferred walk-on spot, and up until he got kicked out of that game, he was going to play at Kent State on scholarship with my son. His dad was the chief of police, and you know how it goes in small towns, if you're connected you never get into any serious trouble.

Anyway, Gary started drinking pretty heavily after the season ended. He barely graduated from high school, and everywhere he went, people were pretty rough on him. High school football is a big deal in Ohio. Once he turned 18, it didn't help him anymore that his dad was the chief of police. People just didn't have patience with him anymore. He got in some trouble for attacking his girlfriend, who was the head cheerleader at the high school. She didn't have to go to the hospital, but she had a black eye and a swollen jaw for awhile. And he pulled some of her hair out, too. Her father ran the meat-packing plant in town, so he was pretty prominent. The two dads worked out a deal where no one would press charges against Gary but he had to stay away from the girl. She was a pretty little thing. Still lives in town. Married a nice kid who sells insurance. Has a couple of kids of her own now. She works part-time at the grocery store where Cheryl and I shop. She knows Vonda is married to Gary, so sometimes the subject comes up when we're checking out at the store. She always tells us she is praying for Vonda, because she knows how violent Gary can be. And when we told her what happened to Vonda this time, she just shook her head and said, "It was just a matter of time, really."

STIll was pretty loyal to Gary, I'll say that for him, and he tried to put him back together. But no one could do that. He was a disaster waiting to happen. He was around the house quite a bit the rest of his senior year and the summer after. The more he got in trouble, the more Vonda got interested in him. My wife came home early from work one day and caught Gary and Vonda in the living room with not much clothing on. This was just a week or two after Gary got in trouble for slapping around that cheerleader. Her name is Mindy, by the way. Mindy Ferguson.

I told Gary if I ever saw him in my house again I'd kill him. And I told Vonda if she ever went with him again she wouldn't ever get any help from me.

Vonda stayed away from him for awhile. She wouldn't go to college, not even the community college over in Logan. She got a bunch of dead-end jobs. Shacked up with a series of losers who took advantage that she was a hard worker and had a good heart. I don't know how many deadbeats she supported while she worked sometimes two or even three jobs. She waitressed, she did temp work, she even worked in warehouses and the meatpacking plant for a while. When she was in her late twenties, she got mixed up with a loser she met at the warehouse where she worked at the time. A sweet talker who just wanted one thing from her. And he got her pregnant with Abbey. He wouldn't marry her, and he wouldn't take responsibility for the baby or her. Still hasn't paid a lick of child support. We took her in for the rest of her pregnancy and took care of her after she had Abbey for a little while.

She got back up on her feet again after a year or two. When Abbey was about two, maybe three, she started seeing Gary again. He had finally gotten his act partially together. Had a high-paying job selling custom machine tools. I say partially together because there were still rumors about him. People said he was still getting into bar fights. Supposedly, he'd had a couple of restraining orders against him from old girlfriends and from businesses.

We told Abbey not to get mixed up with Gary. He was just too violent. STIll took her aside at Thanksgiving and warned her about him and told her he was trouble and no good would come of it. That seemed to make it even worse. She moved in with him. A couple of times after she moved in, we'd keep Abbey for the night, and Abbey would tell us she didn't like Daddy Gary because he was mean to Mommy. And Cheryl noticed some bruises on Vonda's arms and neck a couple of times. Vonda wouldn't answer questions about them.

One day, Vonda and Gary told us they were moving to Calamity City over in the State of Calamity. His work was transferring him. And they went. A year or so later, she was pregnant with little Stanley, and they got married. They got married by a justice of the peace there in Calamity City and told everyone about it later.

At Christmas a few months after they got married—she was still pregnant—they came to our house and stayed with us. Cheryl noticed some bruises again. Vonda seemed different to us. He was totally controlling. She didn't have her own money and had to ask for cash to buy some gifts for Abbey. He wouldn't let her have a credit card.

One night when Gary went out with some of his old buddies, the ones that would still talk to him, I took Vonda aside and told her: "It was a mistake for you to ever marry that man. No good will come of it. The day might come when you need to get away from him." I gave her $1,000 and told her she had to keep it a secret from him, but it would help her get away if she ever needed to. She didn't say anything about Gary, but just gave me a big hug and said "Thanks, Daddy." She had tears in her eyes. That told me everything I needed to know about what was going on in her marriage.

Vonda has her problems, don't get me wrong. She has always been a heavy drinker since she started rebelling in high school. I've talked to her about it and can't get her to stop. She got a DUI here in Freebridge about 10 years ago. And I know she's used other stuff as well—marijuana, pills. But she works hard, and she's a good person at heart. And a great mother. I'll tell you that. Cheryl watches for things like that. Those kids are always wearing good quality, clean clothes. And they're well behaved. And well fed. If something happens to Vonda, I'm going to sue for custody of the kids. I don't want that bastard Gary or his co-dependent parents raising my grandkids.

So, flash forward to the night of the 10th/early morning of the 11th of July, 200x-1. I got a phone call from Vonda. She didn't sound good. She was hysterical, to start off with. She did sound like she might have been intoxicated, but she was so upset it was hard to tell. Crying and wailing. Hyperventilating. I mean, it was something. This high-pitched tone in her voice that was a combination of fear, and sorrow, and rage. All of it. I had to keep asking her to slow down and repeat herself. She was at the hospital. I'll never forget what she told me, because it was the first time in her life she ever said I was right about anything: "You were right, Daddy! He tried to kill me tonight. In front of the kids. I was trying to get away from him. I was going to come home to you and Mommy. He kicked me, and he choked me, and he threw me down on the floor in the garage. There was blood everywhere! And he's got the kids, Daddy! He's got my babies!" I got her calmed down some more and found she had gotten arrested for DUI and they were looking at her for a concussion and other injuries. I told her she should get an order of protection, and I promised to come out there and take care of her.

Well, I called in to work and was able to get some vacation time that was coming to me starting on Tuesday. In the meantime, Cheryl and I packed up the car and got ready to drive to Calamity City.

I wasn't surprised to find out that Gary's mother came and took the kids. His family has always rescued him from everything. I think his parents moved down to Kentucky somewhere after his dad retired. I'm pretty upset about this, and I think Gary and his parents ought to be charged with kidnapping. And Gary ought to be locked up for attempted murder.

I can't figure out what the hell is wrong with this town. A woman gets the hell beaten out of her, and SHE gets charged with domestic battery against a guy the size of Gary? Nothing like this would ever happen in Ohio, I can promise you that. Not even Gary's dad was this corrupt.

Stanley Jones, Jr.

Signed and Sworn

CALAMITY CITY POLICE DEPARTMENT – CASE NO. 11-11-11 DATE 7/12/YEAR-1

STATEMENT OF: Name: Lee Austera DOB: 7/22/Year-46

Address: 4578 Lesar Street, Calamity City, Calamity

Telephone No: 867-5223

I, Lee Austera, have come to the Calamity City Police Department to give a statement in the case of Vonda Fitzpeter. The director of the Women's Shelter called me and asked if I could make a statement, and I agreed to do so. I am an emergency room nurse at the Calamity City Hospital. I was working the evening shift on July 10, 20xx. Most of the evening was relatively uneventful. We had some sick babies come in and a couple of people injured in bar fights near the University. The usual.

Around 10 pm, the paramedics brought in a woman. She was about 5'3" tall, maybe 130 pounds. She looked awful. She was wearing a light-colored blouse, and it was just drenched in blood. There was a big gash on her head, a laceration, and it was bleeding profusely. She had blood matted in her hair and all over her face and shirt.

There was also a police officer there, Sergeant Pelfrey. I thought he was intrusive. As we were trying to get her cleaned up and stabilized, he kept asking her questions and trying to get her to sign a rights waiver.

From what I could gather, she and her husband had gotten into a fight. When I asked her about the laceration on her head, she told me her husband had slammed her head into a concrete floor. She also said that he had choked her and held her down with his knee on her back. I checked her neck and there was some bruising on her neck. She also had a bruise in the small of her back, which she said was from her husband kneeling on her. There were also some red marks on her ribcage. I have looked at the medical records and I know these things are not annotated on them. I do not know why the doctor did not do this.

An unfortunate part of my job is that I see a lot of victims of domestic abuse. And I would have to say that this woman, Vonda Fitzpeter, was the victim of domestic abuse.

I think she is also a victim of the police department. This officer was hovering as we were trying to treat her. She was obviously upset, but he insisted on making her sign a rights waiver so he could interview her. He also had her sign a waiver so we could draw her blood and test it for hallucinogenic mushrooms. She kept telling him the test would prove she hadn't been using mushrooms. And she was right. There was no sign of mushrooms in her blood.

I did not smell alcohol on her breath or person when I was treating her. I know what it smells like, and I have to deal with it all the time in the ER. But I didn't smell any that night. Her speech was slurred, however, and she was in a state of anxiety and high emotion.

The minute the doctor said she was stable enough to be moved, the officer checked her out of the emergency room. She was wearing a hospital gown and we had placed her clothes in a plastic bag for her. He cuffed her and marched her through the emergency room in that gown. She kept trying to make sure it stayed closed.

If I were her, I would sue the Calamity Police Department.

Signed: Lee Austera

EMERGENCY ORDER OF PROTECTION	Court Ph. ___666-987-6543____________________ Court _1st________ JUDICIAL CIRCUIT County _Calamity_ State of CALAMITY Case No. _11-11-111__________________

PETITIONER

_Vonda_____________ A_______________ Fitzpeter_____
First Middle Last

Petitioner's □ Address / □ Alternative Address:

Calamity City Women's Shelter, 1234 Waverly Way ____________________

_Calamity City, Calamity 66666_____

☑ Petitioner
And/or on behalf of other protected person(s) listed below:
☑ Child(ren) as noted on page 6, Part C of this order
☑ Dependent _Abbey Fitzpeter___ (name)
□ High Risk Adult ______________ (name)

RESPONDENT

_Gary______________ L_____________ Fitzpeter______
First Middle Last

Relationship to Petitioner: _Spouse__________________

Respondent's Address:

_8119 Calamity Way_______________ ____________________________________

____________________________________ ____________________________________
(Home) (Work)

Caution Indicators:
□ (A) Considered armed and/or dangerous
□ (S) Suicidal
□ (Y) Considered armed, dangerous and suicidal

RESPONDENT IDENTIFIERS

SEX	RACE	DOB	HT.	WT.
M	W	7-22-YEAR-34	6'3"	250
EYES	HAIR	SOCIAL SECURITY (last 4 #s)		
Hazel	Black			
DRIVER'S LIC. #	STATE	License Plate		

Distinguishing Features (scars, marks, tattoos, martial arts):

______________________ ______________________

____

THE COURT FINDS:
That it has jurisdiction over the Petitioner and subject matter and the Respondent will be provided with reasonable notice and an opportunity to be heard within the timer required by Calamity law.

THE COURT ORDERS: (Additional terms are set forth herein)

☑ That Respondent is prohibited from further acts/threats of abuse on protected persons.
☑ That Respondent is ordered to stay away from Petitioner and/or other protected persons.
☐ That the Circuit Clerk so ordered to send within 24 hours Daycare/School Notice(s). (See page 7)

The terms of this Order shall be effective until 9-2-YEAR-1 (Date) 4:00 pm (Time am/pm)

A hearing on the entry of a Plenary/Interim Order of Protection is set for: 9-2-YEAR-1 (Date) at 9 am (Time)

at the Calamity City Courthouse in Courtroom 1.

A PLENARY (FINAL) ORDER OF PROTECTION MAY BE ENTERED AGAINST YOU BY DEFAULT IF YOU FAIL TO APPEAR AT SUCH HEARING.

FINDINGS [General]

The Court, having reviewed the verified petition and having examined the petitioner under oath or affirmation, finds that:

☑ Venue is proper
☑ The Respondent has abused the Petitioner and/or the child(ren) so identified in this order and/or the protected person(s) listed on this order.
☐ The abused person(s) is/are unable to bring this Petition on his/her own behalf due to age, health, disability or inaccessibility.
☐ The Petition has been filed on behalf of a high-risk adult with disabilities who has been abused, neglected, or exploited by a family or household member.
☐ An Order of Protection has previously been entered in the instant proceeding or in another proceeding in which any party, or a child of any party, or both, has/have been designated as either a respondent or a protected person.

IT IS ORDERED the following remedies that are checked apply in this case.

PART A. REMEDIES INVOLVING PERSONAL PROTECTION

☑ 1. **(R01) (Police Enforced)** With respect to all protected persons, Respondent if prohibited from committing the following acts of abuse or threats of abuse (check all that apply):

☑ Harassment, interference with personal liberty, physical abuse, or stalking.
☑ Intimidation of a dependent.
☐ Willful deprivation.
☐ Neglect.
☐ Exploitation.

☑ 2. **(R03) (Police Enforced) Stay Away**
☑ a. That the Respondent is ordered to stay at least __500___ feet away from the Petitioner and/or protected person(s)' and their residence, school, daycare, employment and any other specified place.

"Stay Away" means for the respondent to refrain from both physical presence and nonphysical contact with the petitioner whether direct, indirect (including, but not limited to, telephone calls, mail, email, faxes, and written notes), or through third parties who may or may not know about the order of protection.

☐ b. Respondent is prohibited from entering or remaining while Petitioner and/or protected person(s) is/are present at:

☐ Their place of residence currently located at ______________________.
☐ Their place of employment at ______________________.
☐ Their school, located at ______________________.
☐ Any of the following specified places, when Petitioner and/or protected person(s) is/are present:
______________________.

☐ 3. **(R14) (Police Enforced)** Respondent is prohibited from entering or remaining in the residence of household while under the influence of drugs or alcohol and constituting a threat to the safety or well-being of Petitioner or Petitioner's children.

PART B. REMEDIES INVOLVING PROPERTY

☐ 1. **(R02) (Police Enforced)** Petitioner is granted exclusive possession of, and Respondent is prohibited from entering or remaining present at the residence/household located at:

____
(Street / P.O. Box) (City) (State) (Zip Code)

☐ Petitioner has a right to occupancy and Respondent has no such right, or
☐ Petitioner and Respondent both have right to occupancy but the balance of hardships favors temporary possession by Petitioner.

☑ 2. **(R10)** (Court Enforced) **Personal Property**
☑ a. Petitioner is granted possession of the following personal property: _personal hygiene products,

clothing, $1,000 cash which was taken from Petitioner by police and given to the Respondent on 7-10-YEAR-1, children's clothing

☐ b. If the Respondent has possession of the property in 2a above, the Respondent shall promptly make it available to the petitioner.

With respect to 2a and 2b above, the Court finds as follows:

☑ The Petitioner, but not the Respondent, owns the property, or

☐ The parties own the property jointly, and sharing it would risk abuse or is impracticable and the balance of hardships favors temporary possession by Petitioner.

☐ c. Respondent is given his/her ☐ clothing ☐ personal adornments ☐ medicine

☐ other personal property, namely ______________________.

☑ 3. **(R10) (Police Enforced)** Personal property shall be transferred

☑ at the residence, or

☐ at ____

(Street) (City) (State) (Zip Code)

That the transfer of personal property shall take place in the presence of:

☐ law enforcement, or ☐ an agreed-upon third party, namely ____________________

☐ Respondent ☐ Petitioner shall have the right to enter the residence to retrieve the property but only in the presence of law enforcement or the designated third party.

Time and date of transfer: within 24 hours of service

(This transfer does not affect title to property)

☐ 4. **(R11)** (Court Enforced) Respondent is prohibited from taking, transferring, concealing, encumbering, damaging, or otherwise disposing of the following real or personal property:

______________________________, except as authorized by the Court because:

☐ Petitioner, but not Respondent, owns the property, or

☐ The parties own the property jointly, and the balance of hardships favors granting this remedy, and/or

☐ Petitioner claims the property as marital property and a proceeding has been filed under the IMDMA.

☐ 5. **(R11)** (Court Enforced) Respondent is prohibited from using financial or other resources of an aged member of the family or household for the profit or advantage of Respondent or any other person.

☐ 6. **(R11.5)** (Court Enforced) That the petitioner is granted the exclusive care, custody, or control of any animal owned, possessed, leashed, kept, or held by either the petitioner or the respondent or a minor child residing in the residence or household of either the petitioner or the respondent and order the respondent to stay away from the animal and forbid the respondent from taking, transferring, encumbering, concealing, harming or otherwise disposing of the animal.

PART C. REMEDIES INVOLVING CHILDREN

The minor child(ren) of the parties is/are:

	Age	State of Residence	Relationship to Petitioner	Included as Protected Party
Stan Fitzpeter	2 1/2		Son	☑
				☐
				☐

☑ 1. The primary caretaker of the minor child(ren) is ☑ Petitioner ☐ Respondent
☐ Other person: ____

☑ 2. **(R05) (Police Enforced)** Petitioner is granted the physical care and possession of the minor child(ren) of the parties, and

☑ a. Respondent is ordered to return the minor children to the physical care of:
☑ Petitioner
☐ Other: ____

on _upon service_______________ at ______________________ am/pm in the presence of ____.

☑ b. Respondent is further ordered not to remove the minor child(ren) from the physical care of the Petitioner, school/school grounds, or babysitter/daycare provider, or other person *in loco parentis.*

☐ c. The Circuit Clerk shall, within 24 hours of the issuance of this Order, send written notice of the Order to any protected child's day care or school to the following: (list child's name and the name and address of each child's school/daycare).

____

____

☐ If this box is checked, the Petitioner shall provide this information to the clerk by a separate written notice which the clerk shall impound to prevent further abuse

☑ 3. **(R07)** (Court Enforced) **Visitation of Minor Child(ren)**

☑ a. Visitation is ☑ **denied** / ☐ **restricted** because Respondent has or is likely to:
☑ Abuse or endanger the minor child(ren) during visitation.
☑ Use visitation as an opportunity to abuse or harass Petitioner, Petitioner's family, or household members
☑ Improperly conceal or detain the minor child(ren).
☑ Act in a manner that is not in the best interest of the minor child(ren).

☑ 4. **(R08) (Police Enforced)** Respondent is ordered not to conceal the minor child(ren) within the State or remove the child(ren) from the State of Calamity.

PART D. MISCELLANEOUS REMEDIES

☑ **(R17)** Respondent is further ordered and enjoins as follows:

1. Any and all attempts at communication or contact will be considered harassment.

2. Respondent is ordered to return Abbey Jones to Petitioner immediately upon service – Respondent is not the biological father of Abbey Jones, has nod adopted her, and has no parental right with respect to Abbey Jones.

THIS EMERGENCY ORDER WAS ISSUED ON: Date: 7-12-YEAR-1

Time: 10 am am/pm

Lionel Parker

JUDGE

I hereby certify that this is a true and correct copy of the original order on file with the court.

____

Clerk of the Circuit Court of

__________________ County, Calamity

Date: __________________________

Investigative Resources, LLC
1914 August Lane
Calamity City, Calamity 66666

October 15, YEAR-1

Findley and Howard, PC
Attn: Vonda Fitzpeter Defense Team
1918 Versailles Blvd.
Calamity City, Calamity 66666

Re: Report of Investigation into July 10 Arrest of Vonda Fitzpeter

Dear Defense Team,

Thank you again for retaining Investigative Resources, LLC, to examine the facts and circumstances surrounding the July 10 arrest of Vonda Fitzpeter for DUI, Child Endangerment, and Domestic Battery. You asked us to examine the following: (1) personal relationships, if any, between Gary Fitzpeter and the arresting officers; (2) what happened to the physical evidence seized from the vehicle and photographs taken at the scene; (3) Gary Fitzpeter's reputation and history in Freebridge, Ohio; and (4) Gary Fitzpeter's current domestic arrangements. This report will address each of the areas in turn.

1. Personal Relationships Between Gary Fitzpeter and Arresting Officers

I interviewed Officer Tracy Taylor and Officer Pat Pelfrey separately on September 5, YEAR-1. Both officers are members of Ducks, Bucks & Brews, a hunting club out in Calamity County. They have known each other for about more than ten years. They both met Fitzpeter when he moved to Calamity City from Freebridge, Ohio, about three years ago. They met him at a club-sponsored skeet shoot right after he became a club member. The three friends regularly hunt and fish together at the club. Taylor and Fitzpeter have taken club-sponsored hunting trips together to South Dakota, Louisiana, and Florida. Taylor and Fitzpeter did not know each other in high school; they grew up in different states and only met three years ago.

The three are also part of a regular poker game involving members of the club. All three have hosted poker games for the group at their homes on multiple occasions. Taylor and Pelfrey remembered Vonda from the games at the Fitzpeter home. They said she was a pleasant hostess who did a good job with the food. Taylor, however, said that she drank heavily and was "embarrassing" when intoxicated. He recounted an incident where Vonda picked a fight with Gary in front of everyone and slapped him.

Officer Taylor wanted me to know that as a professional law enforcement officer, he would never let a personal relationship interfere with his law enforcement duties. Officer Pelfrey expressed the same sentiments when I met with him.

Both men denied receiving a personal cell phone call from Gary Fitzpeter the night of the incident, but in my opinion neither man had a good explanation for how they both ended up at 513 Fremont at the same time and just as Vonda Fitzpeter arrived at a friend's house. Taylor, who claimed not to know Tiffany Clarke, said he was patrolling in the area and went there on a hunch. Pelfrey said the dispatcher told him to assist another officer in the Fremont area.

The chief was not aware that Gary belonged to Ducks, Bucks, and Brews or that Gary hunted and played poker with the two officers. He did not feel that it would have affected their ability to investigate the case, however. He said, "In a town this small, that's kind of what you have to deal with. Everyone knows everyone. And who *isn't* part of a poker game somewhere?" He advised that everyone who was anyone in Calamity County—including himself—belonged to Ducks, Bucks, and Brews. "I don't know the man personally," he said, referring to Gary, "but I've probably sat in a duck blind with him."

2. Physical Evidence and Digital Photographs of Incident

The police report indicated that some physical evidence, including two bottles of alcohol and a bag of what appeared to be hallucinogenic mushrooms, was destroyed. During the September 5 interview, Officer Pelfrey admitted to destroying the evidence by emptying the bottles and putting them into recycling. He said he flushed the mushrooms down the toilet at the police station. He advised that this was because after the BAC results came back, the case was open and shut and there was no need to pile on by adding open container charges. Taylor said he was aware that Pelfrey had destroyed the evidence, but advised that it was an unwritten department policy to destroy alcohol and drug evidence because the evidence room technician had some problems with substance abuse and the chief didn't want that kind of evidence to tempt the tech.

I visited the police station on September 6, YEAR-1, and spoke to the chief who denied that such a policy existed. The chief was unable to provide me with any written evidence retention or destruction policies, or any written policies at all. According to him, the department is not big enough to require written policies and things "run pretty well around here" under his supervision as chief. He would not allow me to see the evidence room or meet the evidence technician. He did not feel it was inappropriate to destroy the evidence in this case, given its open and shut nature and Vonda's intoxication level.

Both of the arresting officers recalled Vonda claiming that Gary had planted the bottles in the car, but they felt she was too intoxicated to be credible and so did not follow up on her claims. Both officers expressed that in her condition, she was a threat to public safety, and advised me not to lose sight of that fact. Officer Taylor advised that "Gary would NEVER do something stupid like plant evidence. He's a stand-up guy." Officer Pelfrey said, "If you listen to her, she didn't know anything was in the car. Not the kid. Not the bottles. Not the meds. Not the mushrooms. Did you ask her if SHE was in the car?"

Officer Pelfrey took digital photographs with their personal cellphones. The officer claimed this was pursuant to department policy. The chief advised that proper procedure (unwritten, of course) is to call the dispatcher and request a photographer, but for relatively minor incidents such as this one, most officers just use their cellphones because it is faster than waiting for the photographer to arrive. The unofficial department policy is to email the pictures to the chief's official email account so he can print them and put them in the case file. The chief acknowledged that this did not happen in this case. He said he did not know why.

Pelfrey claimed to have upgraded phones about a month after the incident and lost all of the pictures, contacts, and data because the clerk at the phone store inadvertently did a hard reset of his old phone while trying to transfer everything over to the new phone. Pelfrey claimed to be quite upset, because the phone had personal pictures on it, including pictures from Pelfrey's sister's August wedding. "Those were the only pictures taken at the wedding," claimed Pelfrey. "The photographer never showed up."

3. Gary Fitzpeter's Reputation and History in Freebridge, Ohio

On September 15 and 16, YEAR-1, I traveled to Freebridge, Ohio, to gather information about Gary Fitzpeter. As a former star high school football player on a team that made it to the state quarterfinals, he was still well known in the area. He had no arrest record in the Freebridge area. And he had no arrest records in the NCIC system. A clerk at the courthouse, speaking on condition of anonymity, said that Gary had been a real troublemaker in his youth but was protected by his father, the police chief in Freebridge at the time, from consequences. The clerk said he was violent and had beaten up a cheerleader at the school. Several community members told me that the team had lost the quarterfinal game when Gary committed a personal foul on the opposing team and then punched a referee. No one seemed surprised to learn that he beat up Vonda. "That's the kind of guy he is," said the courthouse clerk. "He's a bully." I located the cheerleader, Mindy Ferguson, who works as a checkout clerk at a grocery store. She declined to speak to me about Gary. I asked if she could confirm that he was a violent person and she said yes. Then she asked me to leave.

There were no orders of protection against him filed at the courthouse.

4. <u>Gary Fitzpeter's Current Domestic Arrangements</u>

Gary filed for divorce from Vonda on August 15 YEAR-1. They are separated pending divorce. Vonda is living in an apartment in Calamity City and has primary physical custody of the children. The Order of Protection against Gary remains in place. Gary has supervised visitation every other weekend. The visitation is supervised by his mother, who brought the children back from Kentucky when she was served with a copy of the Order of Protection that granted custody to Vonda.

Gary is still living in the marital residence. A local woman, Fay Nolan, stage name Betsey Divine, often stays at the house over the weekends. She is in her early 30's and works two jobs as a waitress at Denny's and as a dancer at the Frisky Pony, a gentleman's club on the Strip in Calamity City. She would not talk to me when I visited her at the Frisky Pony and asked security to escort me out. When I asked her if she knew Gary she said it was none of my business. As security was escorting me out she volunteered that "Vonda is a whore and she's going to lose her kids once she gets convicted of everything."

Sincerely,

Franklin Irving

Franklin Irving
Investigative Resources, LLC
"We'll find out. That's our promise."

Jury Instructions

Pretrial Instructions

Members of the jury, the trial is about to commence, and I now will instruct you as to the law regarding some of your duties during trial and deliberations.

You should not do any independent investigation or research on any subject or person relating to the case. What you may have seen or heard outside the courtroom is not evidence. This includes any press, radio, or television programs and it also includes any information available on the Internet. Such programs, reports, and information are not evidence and your verdict must not be influenced in any way by such material.

For example, you must not use the Internet or any other sources to search for any information about the case, or the law which applies to the case.

During the course of the trial, do not communicate with, provide information personally, in writing, or electronically to anyone about this case – not even your own families or friends, courtroom personnel, and also not even among yourselves until instructed otherwise.

Lawyers, parties, and witnesses are not permitted to speak with you about any subject, even if unrelated to this case, until after the case is over and you are discharged from your duties as jurors.

Final Instructions

Members of the jury, the evidence and arguments in this case have been completed, and I now will instruct you as to the law.

The law that applies to this case is stated in these instructions, and it is your duty to follow all of them. You must not single out certain instructions and disregard others. When I use the word "he" in these instructions, I mean a male or a female.

It is your duty to determine the facts and to determine them only from the evidence in this case. You are to apply the law to the facts and in this way decide the case.

Neither sympathy nor prejudice should influence you. You should not be influenced by any person's race, color, religion, or national ancestry.

From time to time it has been the duty of the court to rule on the admissibility of evidence. You should not concern yourselves with the reasons for these rulings. You should disregard questions and exhibits which were withdrawn or to which objections were sustained.

Any evidence that was received for a limited purpose should not be considered by you for any other purpose.

You should disregard testimony and exhibits which the court has refused or stricken.

The evidence which you should consider consists only of the testimony of the witnesses and the exhibits which the court has received.

Opening statements are made by the attorneys to acquaint you with the facts they expect to prove. Closing arguments are made by the attorneys to discuss the facts and circumstances in the case and should be confined to the evidence and to reasonable inferences to be drawn from the evidence. Neither opening statements nor closing arguments are evidence, and any statement or argument made by the attorneys which is not based on the evidence should be disregarded.

Those of you who took notes during trial may use your notes to refresh your memory during jury deliberations.

Each juror should rely on his or her recollection of the evidence. Just because a juror has taken notes does not necessarily mean that his or her recollection of the evidence is any better or more accurate than the recollection of a juror who did not take notes.

When you are discharged from further service in this case, your notes will be collected by the deputy and destroyed. Throughout that process, your notes will remain confidential and no one will be allowed to see them.

You should consider all the evidence in the light of your own observations and experience in life.

Neither by these instructions nor by any ruling or remark which I have made do I mean to indicate any opinion as to the facts or as to what your verdict should be.

Faithful performance by you of your duties as jurors is vital to the administration of justice.

Only you are the judges of the believability of the witnesses and of the weight to be given to the testimony of each of them. In considering the testimony of any witness, you may take into account his ability and opportunity to observe, his age, his memory, his manner while testifying, any interest, bias, or prejudice he may have, and the reasonableness of his testimony considered in the light of all the evidence in the case.

The believability of a witness may be challenged by evidence that on some former occasion he made a statement or acted in a manner that was not consistent with his testimony in this case. Evidence of this kind ordinarily may be considered by you only for the limited purpose of deciding the weight to be given the testimony you heard from the witness in this courtroom.

You have before you evidence that the defendant made statements relating to the offense charged in the indictment. It is for you to determine whether the defendant made the statements, and, if so, what weight should be given to the statements. In determining the weight to be given to a statement, you should consider all of the circumstances under which it was made.

You should judge the testimony of the defendant in the same manner as you judge the testimony of any other witness.

Circumstantial evidence is the proof of facts or circumstances which give rise to a reasonable inference of other facts which tend to show the guilt or innocence of the defendant. Circumstantial evidence should be considered by you together with all the other evidence in the case in arriving at your verdict.

The defendant is charged with the offenses of domestic battery, driving under the influence of alcohol, and endangering the life and health of a child. The defendant has pleaded not guilty.

The charges against the defendant in this case are contained in a document called the information. This document is the formal method of charging the defendant and placing the defendant on trial. It is not any evidence against the defendant.

The defendant is presumed to be innocent of the charges against her. This presumption remains with her throughout every stage of the trial and during your deliberations on the verdict and is not overcome unless from all the evidence in this case you are convinced beyond a reasonable doubt that he is guilty.

The State has the burden of proving the guilt of the defendant beyond a reasonable doubt, and this burden remains on the State throughout the case. The defendant is not required to prove her innocence. (IF APPLICABLE) The fact that the defendant did not testify must not be considered by you in any way in arriving at your verdict.

Charge I: Domestic Battery

A person commits the offense of domestic battery when she knowingly and by any means causes bodily harm to any family or household member.

The phrase "family or household member" means spouses, former spouses, parents, children, stepchildren, persons related by blood or marriage, persons who share or formerly shared a common dwelling, persons who allegedly have a child in common, persons who allegedly share a blood relationship through a child, persons who have or have had a dating or engagement relationship, and persons with disabilities and their personal assistants.

To sustain the charge of domestic battery, the State must prove the following propositions:

First Proposition: That the defendant knowingly caused bodily harm to Gary Fitzpeter; and

Second Proposition: That Gary Fitzpeter was then a family or household member to the defendant.

Third Proposition: That the defendant was not justified in using the force which she used.

If you find from your consideration of all the evidence that each one of these propositions has been proved beyond a reasonable doubt, you should find the defendant guilty of that charge.

If you find from your consideration of all the evidence that any one of these propositions has not been proved beyond a reasonable doubt, you should find the defendant not guilty of that charge.

If you find from your consideration of all the evidence that each one of these propositions has been proved beyond a reasonable doubt, you should find the defendant guilty of that charge.

If you find from your consideration of all the evidence that any one of these propositions has not been proved beyond a reasonable doubt, you should find the defendant not guilty of that charge.

In this case the State must prove beyond a reasonable doubt the proposition that the defendant was not justified in using the force which she used.

The phrases “reasonable belief” or “reasonably believes” mean that the person concerned, acting as a reasonable person, believes that the described facts exist.

A person is justified in the use of force when and to the extent that she reasonably believes that such conduct is necessary to defend herself against the imminent use of unlawful force.

Charge Two: Driving with an Alcohol Concentration of 0.08 or More

A person commits the offense of driving with an alcohol concentration of 0.08 or more when he knowingly and understandingly drives or is in actual physical control of a vehicle while the alcohol concentration in his blood or breath is 0.08 or more.

The term “alcohol concentration” means either grams of alcohol per 100 milliliters of blood or grams of alcohol per 210 liters of breath. Alcohol concentration may be determined by analysis of a person's breath, blood, urine, or other bodily substance.

The phrase “actual physical control” means that the defendant was in the vehicle and in a position to exercise control over the vehicle by starting the engine and causing the vehicle to move.

To sustain the charge of driving with an alcohol concentration of 0.08 or more, the State must prove the following propositions:

First Proposition: That the defendant knowingly and understandingly drove or was in actual physical control of a vehicle; and

Second Proposition: That at the time the defendant drove or was in actual physical control of a vehicle, the alcohol concentration in the defendant's blood or breath was 0.08 or more; and

Third Proposition: That the defendant did not act out of necessity.

If you find from your consideration of all the evidence that each one of these propositions has been proved beyond a reasonable doubt, you should find the defendant guilty.

If you find from your consideration of all the evidence that any one of these propositions has not been proved beyond a reasonable doubt, you should find the defendant not guilty.

In this case, the parties have stipulated that the defendant’s alcohol concentration in both blood and breath was 0.17.

Conduct which would otherwise be an offense is justifiable by reason of necessity if the defendant was without blame in occasioning or developing the situation and reasonably believed that such conduct was necessary to avoid a public or private injury greater than the injury which might reasonably result from his own conduct.

Charge Three: Endangering the Life or Health of a Child

A person commits the offense of endangering the life or health of a child when she has the care or custody of a child and knowingly or understandingly causes or permits that child to be placed in such a situation that the child's life or health may be endangered.

To sustain the charge of endangering the life or health of a child, the State must prove the following propositions:

First Proposition: That the defendant had the care or custody of Abbey Jones; and

Second Proposition: That the defendant knowingly or understandingly caused or permitted Abbey Jones to be placed in such a situation that endangered the life or health of Abbey Jones; and

Third Proposition: That the defendant did not act out of necessity.

If you find from your consideration of all the evidence that each one of these propositions has been proved beyond a reasonable doubt, you should find the defendant guilty.

If you find from your consideration of all the evidence that any one of these proposition has not been proved beyond a reasonable doubt, you should find the defendant not guilty.

Conduct which would otherwise be an offense is justifiable by reason of necessity if the defendant was without blame in occasioning or developing the situation and reasonably believed that such conduct was necessary to avoid a public or private injury greater than the injury which might reasonably result from his own conduct.

When you retire to the jury room you first will elect one of your members as your foreperson. He or she will preside during your deliberations on your verdict.

Your agreement on a verdict must be unanimous. Your verdict must be in writing and signed by all of you, including your foreperson.

The defendant is charged with the offenses of domestic battery, driving under the influence of alcohol, and endangering the life or health of a child. As to each charge, you will be provided with both a "not guilty" and "guilty" choice on the verdict form. As to each charge, circle the selection that represents the unanimous choice of the jury. Then the foreperson and all jurors must sign the form. Your signature acknowledges that the verdict accurately reflects your choice.

Verdict Form

Charge One: Domestic Battery

We, the jury, find the defendant, Vonda Fitzpeter, not guilty / guilty of domestic battery.

Charge Two: Driving Under the Influence

We, the jury, find the defendant, Vonda Fitzpeter, not guilty / guilty of driving with an alcohol concentration of 0.08 or more.

Charge Three: Endangering the Life and Health of a Child

We, the jury, find the defendant, Vonda Fitzpeter, not guilty / guilty of endangering the life and health of a child.

Signed this ____ day of _______, YEAR

____

Foreperson

____

____

____

____

____

____

____

____

____

____

COPYRIGHT

PEOPLE V. FITZPETERS

First Edition
PDF & Print Edition (c) May 2014

ISBN-10:0989666727
ISBN-13: 978-0-9896667-2-5

PUBLISHER

Practice Ready Press
A Subdivision of CHR Publishing
United States
CHR Publishing
6261 14th Avenue South
Suite 201
Gulfport, Florida 33707
Phone: 813-924-4717

Printed in Dunstable, United Kingdom

91218887R00047